25 CYCLE

EDINBURGH
AND
LOTHIAN

D1459310

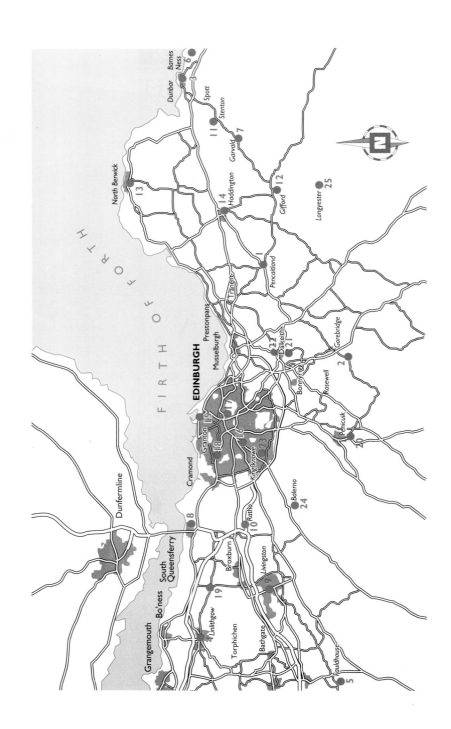

25 CYCLE ROUTES

EDINBURGH AND LOTHIAN

Derek Purdy

With a Foreword by the CTC

EDINBURGH:HMSO

First published 1996

Applications for reproduction should be made to HMSO

Also available in this series: *25 Cycle Routes – In and Around Glasgow*

Acknowledgements

HMSO acknowledges with thanks the valuable advice from Lothian
Regional Council Transportation Department staff,. Thanks are also due to
Derek Purdy and Paul Watt of HMSO Photography for access to and
use of transparencies.

British Library Cataloguing in Publication Data

A catalogue record for this book is available from the British Library

ISBN 0 11 495717 7

CONTENTS

FOREWORD BY THE CTC

Cycling is healthy, environmentally-friendly – and above all fun! Travel at your own pace, meet people along the way and experience the real country. Explore parts of the country that you didn't know existed – and improve your fitness at the same time! Cycling is good for you, so go by bike, and you'll feel a whole lot better for it!

Safety considerations and equipment needed

• A few days before you plan to go cycling, check your bike thoroughly for broken, worn and/or loose parts. In particular, check for worn tyres and broken/loose spokes. Ensure that both brakes and the gear system are working well, with the chain lightly oiled and running smoothly. If in doubt, your local bike shop will be able to advise further. Better to fix anything now, than to spoil your cycle ride later! Low gears will be useful for any hills or strong winds.

• Carry a cycle lock and key and a small tool kit (spare inner tube, tyre levers, small adjustable spanner, puncture repair outfit, pump and allen keys if your bike needs them).

• If possible, luggage should be carried on the bike, not on your back, although you should be able to fit everything you need into an expanding bumbag. A rear carrying rack is useful. Ideally, pack everything into plastic bags inside a saddlebag or panniers, which are properly secured to this rack. Ensure that when "loaded" your luggage is well balanced, and that its weight doesn't affect your steering/handling of the bike. Check that nothing will fall into your wheels.

• Always carry food and water, for example sandwiches, biscuits and a full water bottle. Cyclists are advised to eat and drink "little and often".

• Comfortable clothing which allows freedom of movement is recommended, and for colder weather take warm clothing: two or three layers (a T-shirt and long-sleeved jerseys) are best. You can take off a layer or two once you've warmed-up and put them back on again if you stop or if it

METRIC MEASUREMENTS

At the beginning of each route, the distance is given in miles and kilometres. Within the text, all measurements are metric for simplicity (and indeed our Ordnance Survey maps are now all metric). However, it was felt that a conversion table might be useful to those readers who, like the author, still tend to think in Imperial terms.

The basic statistic to remember is that one kilometre is five-eighths of a mile. Half a mile is equivalent to 800 metres and a quarter-mile is 400 metres. Below that distance, yards and metres are little different in practical terms.

km	miles
1	0.625
1.6	1
2	1.25
3	1.875
3.2	2
4	2.5
4.8	3
5	3.125
6	3.75
6.4	4
7	4.375
8	5
9	5.625
10	6.25
16	10

gets cold. Several layers allow precise temperature control. It is also a good idea to carry wet-weather gear and/or a wind-proof garment if the weather looks as if it may turn bad. A peaked cap can help protect your eyes from rain and wind, helping you to see where you're going! For hot weather don't forget your sun cream and sunglasses!

You don't have to wear specialist cycling clothing to enjoy cycling – wear what you feel comfortable in. Padded shorts, gloves, cycling shoes, cycle helmets and much more can be purchased at cycle shops if you're interested. N.B. It is not compulsory to wear a helmet, and the choice is yours. The CTC can provide further information on helmets if needed.

- Check that your riding position is comfortable. Saddle height: when seated, place your heel on the pedal when it is at its lowest point. Your leg should be straight, and your knee just off the locked position. On the subject of riding comfort, many bikes are supplied with saddles designed for men (long and narrow). Women may prefer to use a woman's saddle (shorter and wider at the back). These are available from bike shops.

- There is some useful advice and information given for cyclists in the Highway Code. This is available from garages, bookshops and may be found in your library.

- If you think that you may be cycling when it is dark, you will need to fit front and rear lights (this is a legal requirement). Lights and reflectors/ reflective band/jacket are also useful in bad weather conditions.

- In the event of an accident, it is advisable to note the time and place of the incident, the names and addresses of those involved, details of their insurance company, any vehicle registration numbers and details of any witnesses present. In the event of injury or damage, report the accident to the police immediately.

- Some of the routes in this book use off-road paths which are shared with pedestrians. Please be courteous and friendly to people you meet and give way to walkers if necessary. A bicycle bell is useful for warning others of your approach.

For further information about cycling . . .

The CTC (Cyclist's Touring Club) is Britain's largest cycling organisation, and can provide a wealth of information and advice about all aspects of cycling. The CTC works on behalf of *all* cyclists to promote cycling and to protect cyclists' interests.

Join the CTC and enjoy *free* third-party insurance, legal aid, touring and technical information, a bi-monthly magazine and a cyclists' handbook. The CTC also organises an annual holiday programme, co-ordinates National Bike Week, runs a wide-ranging and effective network of cycle campaigners and holds weekly cycle rides all over the country.

For details of these, and our many other services, contact the CTC at: Cotterell House, 69 Meadrow, Godalming, Surrey GU7 3HS, or telephone 01483 417217, fax 01483 426994.

INTRODUCTION

This guide has two intentions. First and foremost to encourage those who are new to cycling, those who have not ridden a bike for a long time, or those who think they might like cycling, to go out and do it. Second it is designed to get you into virtually every corner of the Lothians. This applies especially to those who have lived for many years in one particular district, but never explored others.

Lothian is a beautiful region, every area having a lot to offer, from the hills to the coast and everything in between. The regional and district authorities have created many cycle facilities, and it is only right that they should feature large in a guide of this type. They are arguably the best in the country.

There are short routes, most of which are predominantly traffic free, railway routes which are totally devoid of steep gradients, the occasional canal route which is completely flat but invariably has a hilly little road to complement it, and a ride to the highest tarmac road in Lothian. Start small and work your way up. They are all enjoyable if you take your time.

Opposite: Cycle path following a picturesque stretch of the Union Canal.

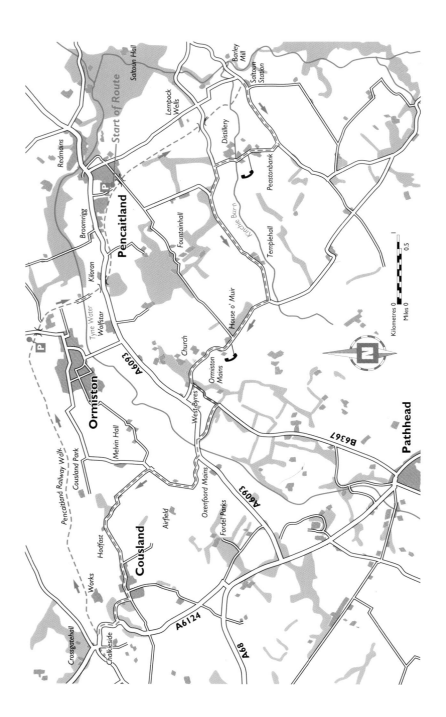

PENCAITLAND RAILWAY

This is a circular tour of the tiny East Lothian coalfield, something missed by motorists, afforded to cyclists by the Pencaitland Railway Path. Railways always provide a different aspect to the countryside, cutting through in fairly straight lines as they do, and, especially in the days of the steam train, were noted havens for wildlife. Occasional trackside fires caused by errant sparks were an accepted hazard, and while they blighted a stretch for a time, the vegetation soon returned to normal, or even grew anew with tremendous vigour.

Nowadays this trackside is actively managed to encourage a great variety of wildlife, probably even more varied than ever, due to its many years of abandonment. Over 90 species of birds have been recorded, which you cannot expect to see all in one day, but even before you leave the car park you will probably notice blue tits, coal tits, yellow hammers and the inevitable sparrows that haunt the grain silos. Once onto the old line you will see scuttling blackbirds scratching among the fallen leaves, and hawks loitering on an elevated perch for the next meal. Mice and voles are plentiful, if not immediately obvious, and you will be well advised to watch out for recent hazardous holes dug by rabbits or even badgers. Spring flowers are augmented by apple and cherry blossom, gorse, broom, willow and rowan or mountain ash, while later in the year you may find wild strawberries and incredible banksides of purple rosebay willowherb between the bridges near Milton House.

The line closed in 1964 when the last mine in the area closed. Passenger services had been withdrawn in 1933, probably because the workforce either lived very close to the pit or within walking or biking distance. Traditionally the railway was the main thoroughfare in mining areas; every railway had a path alongside used by both pedestrians and cyclists, and even on a Sunday the locals used it as the route to visit relatives. It was usually the most direct line of communication, so you

INFORMATION

Distance: 21.8 km (13.5 miles).

Map: OS Landranger, sheet 66.

Start and finish: Site of Pencaitland Station.

Terrain: Nearly half of the route, 9.1 km (5.7 miles), is on railway path, all of which is good when dry, but in wet conditions can provide some soft strenuous stretches suitable only for mountain bikes. The remainder of the route is tarmac.

Refreshments: None en route. Picnic recommended.

Classic East Lothian County Council fingerpost of considerable vintage.

will see that a shared facility is nothing new, but please treat other users with due consideration.

The car park at the start of the route is situated beside the huge grain silos at the west end of Pencaitland village, to the south of the A6093 road. Access is via a bumpy road down the side of the silo site, the entrance being marked by a blue cycleway fingerpost announcing 'Ormiston 2 Saltoun 2'.

Depart south-east towards Saltoun. Despite the fact that you could rightly have expected the railway to be level, a little gradient post indicates a 1 in 50 climb to start. Opposite the last bungalow of Pencaitland a tombstone plaque marks the site of the most south-easterly mine in the Haddington area. Nothing now remains; in fact were it not for the reminder you would never think this place had been anything other than the vast field it now is.

The cutting you now enter hosts the best possibility of dampness due to the lie of the land and tree cover; there may also be a corresponding increase in effort required to ride. Children will love the challenge.

Lothian beeches near Saltoun Station.

The rosebay willowherb banksides now feature between the bridges, then suddenly you reach the end of the line at Saltoun Station. Turn right up the hill past beech hedges, then right again at the first opportunity towards a chimney that looks like the neck of a bottle, but it is no coincidence, you are bound for the Glenkinchie distillery. The home of the amber nectar looks like a model factory nestling in the vale of the Kinchie Burn. If you pass between 0930 and 1600, Monday to Friday, you may be tempted to join a guided tour!

Westwards with the Kinchie Burn to the B6371 then to the north past House o' Muir, where turnips were first grown in drills, thus solving the problem of winter feeding for cattle, now with a cottage sporting four large solar panels on the roof. Still at the forefront of technology! Immediately beyond the burn at West Byres turn left onto a very narrow road which will considerably reduce the length of the A6093 to be traversed en route to Cousland. Take great care on the short stretch of main road, turning right at the black and white Armco barriers after crossing the bridge over the Tyne Water.

The road to Cousland is signposted beyond the Airfield road end, and is steep. A good time to dismount with the excuse of admiring the countryside. A tiny downhill from the west end of the village then takes you down to the A6124, where you turn right at the civil amenity site, posh for dump, but displaying colliery tubs bonnier than they ever were in their working days, for the final 500 m of tarmac before the railway run for home.

By turning left onto the B6414 one gets to Thorny Bank and Route 22 to Musselburgh. This is Crossgatehall. Initially the path is well surfaced but narrows as you progress. Then it comes into sight: the pitheap, the biggest visible remains of the coalfield. More 'tombstones' record the sites of the pits. You'll probably be surprised how close together they lie. One reads: 'Oxenford Pit (Ormiston Coal Co.). Sunk 1907 re-sunk 1909 abandoned 1932. Output before closure 250/300 tons a day. Smeaton 2.6 miles.'

The "tombstone" commemorating Ormiston Station Pit.

Beyond the main colliery site the countryside becomes more open and there is a splendid bridge over the line. Look in the embankment off to the right: there is a beautiful dressed stone culvert for the little burn nearly hidden by wild vegetation, but check the outlet at the far side, it is somewhat less grand.

There are now no mining connections at Ormiston apart from railway paraphernalia hidden in the hedges near the grain silos and a pair of rails embedded in the tiny sewerage works road you cross before the final uphill to the A6093 again. You will not need any reminder to pause at the top, from where you can see the Pencaitland silos. All that remains is a pleasant sweep around to the old station, so close to the main road but totally divorced from it. For the sake of 50 m you are back in the heart of the country.

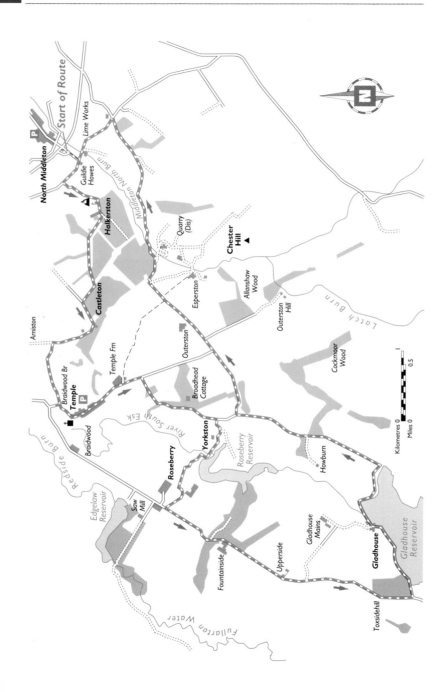

Start of Route

North Middleton

Lime Works

Guildie Howes

Middleton North Burn

Halkerston

Quarry (Dis)

Chester Hill

Castleton

Esperston

Allanshaw Wood

Outerston Hill

Latch Burn

Arniston

Temple Fm

Outerston

Cockmoor Wood

Braidwood Br

Temple

Broadhead Cottage

River South Esk

Yorkston

Roseberry Reservoir

Howburn

Braidwood

Roseberry

Redside Burn

Edgelaw Reservoir

Saw Mill

Fountainside

Upperside

Gladhouse Mains

Gladhouse

Gladhouse Reservoir

Toxsidehill

Fullarton Water

Kilometres 0   0.5   1

Miles 0

MOORFOOT RESERVOIRS

his ride is long and very hilly within the context of this book, but the rewards are high. Even on a bitterly cold day in early January it was a great tour, albeit with a certain amount of excitement generated by sheets of ice covering the entire road in a couple of places!

Invariably you find reservoirs in high and remote places; Gladhouse and Rosebery are no exception, but these large sheets of water seem totally at home nestling beneath the Moorfoot Hills, as if they'd always been there. The Moorfoot, or Muirfoot, Hills dominate the southern skyline of the tour, and should you look down on this area from their heights it would seem reasonably flat. This is far from the truth, the route rises and falls in a very localised manner, quite severely on occasions.

Do not be put off by the heights on the map, the ride starts 200 m above sea level. Depart south-west towards the lime works then right up the hill at Guildie Howes and first left up an even steeper hill towards Halkerston. The surface of this sustained hill is quite rough for tarmac and the gradient is sufficient to produce immediate warmth in the winter, or have you reaching for the water bottle on a summer day. The rabbits take their time getting out of the way; they know you will not be travelling very fast.

Look left as you crest the summit beyond the farm and you will see a transmission mast hidden by the trees; look ahead and the Pentlands don't seem so big, the main reason being you are now 260 m above sea level. If you pause and turn around you will see the Hartside Hill mast above Oxton in the next county.

A simple hide by the little pond above Castleton suggested there could be duck thereabouts but an enormous flock of woodpigeon, 300 or more, was the predominant sight as it lifted off the winter neeps.

INFORMATION

Distance: 25.9 km (16.1 miles).

Map: OS Landranger, sheet 66.

Start and finish: North Middleton, old road SW of A7(T). There is more room on the far side of the A7, but exercise great care crossing the main road.

Terrain: All tarmac. Quiet byroads, some single track.

Refreshments: None en route. Middleton Inn at start and finish: pub grub.

The heraldic beasts adorning pillars of the gates of Arniston.

Timber Cottage and one of the most organised and professional-looking sawmills in Lothian are passed en route to the B6372, but take time to inspect the ornate southern gates of Arniston before shooting off towards Temple. Can you decipher the date incorporated in the design, and how would you describe the beasts atop the pillars? They seem more heraldic than realistic. The road along to Braidwood Bridge is fairly quiet despite its status, the only vehicle passing being a huge Fire Brigade turntable ladder! Take time for a mini diversion onto the bridge; it will also give you a breather before the long pull up through Temple. The noise strikes one immediately: it is coming from the weir on the downstream side. The water looks clean and fresh, confirmed by an old heron that circled 360 degrees then floated off into the trees of Braidwood. Herons are a good barometer of the condition of the local waters: they do not hang around if there are no fish, and there are few fish that can abide pollution.

The overflow cascades at Rosebery reservoir.

Take your time up the hill through Temple: the cottage architecture both old and new is worth a look, and if you are very observant you will see the little school hidden away behind the main street. Over the top of the hill and beyond the dip, turn right at the sign for Rosebery, but alas it is up a bit more. You turn right for Rosebery Reservoir before the hilltop cottages with their tiny coal-houses at the opposite side of the road, and weave down through Yorkston Farm, where the stackyard was a sea of turnips, first-rate winter fodder.

The first sight of the reservoir you get is the tip of the eastern arm, then an ever-tightening right hander takes you down onto the dam, where it is imperative you stop and admire the place. The grounds are beautifully kept. There was a raft of mallard on the southern arm and a remarkable pattern as the water lapped over the spillway. In reservoir terms Rosebery is not big, but the keeper once saw a roe deer stag swim all the way across the widest part, come ashore at 'the tree', leap the fence and quietly walk off up the road totally unconcerned. Quite a feat. Geese now breed on Edgelaw Reservoir a kilometre to the north-west.

There is a further stretch of the B6372 past Fountainside then follow the sign for Gladhouse onto a lesser road. Limekilns of varying vintage provide roadside interest but their only current function seems to be rubbish-burning sites and the biggest rabbit burrows in the land. Toxsidehill (290 m) is the highest point on your route, but do not get carried away on the downhill because you turn left at the bottom for Gladhouse Reservoir.

Even in the depth of winter Gladhouse is a bonnie place; all it needs is a little weak sun and the water comes alive.

There are two car parks with adjacent banksides, which will make excellent sites for a break, but the wind was freshening and it was a case of dining standing up! However, there was a bonus. Standing at the eastern wall where the Black Burn enters, it was intriguing to watch the wind-blown

Ancient limekiln near Toxidehill.

ripples die out under the ice, the sheet of which appeared quite thick, only to reappear 40 or 50 m later at the dam wall, where there were a few inches of clear water, and wash back out on top of the ice to freeze.

Now starts the run for home. Narrow roads all the way. Initially north past Howburn, set some distance back across the fields, then north-east past Outerston, then east through the quarries to Middleton. Sheets of ice lay completely covering the road in the lanes near Esperston, but it was no problem for the mountain bike, which rode the verge with ease. There is an unusual brick bridge across the Middleton North Burn and a ruinous limestone quarry building as you climb the hill beyond. The jungle is claiming the countryside back with a vengeance at these outermost workings, but as you reach the top of the hill you will see the extraction goes on. A huge gorge has been dug in this good-quality limestone over the years, and your vantage point high on the hillside road gives an excellent impression of the scale of the operation. At Middleton crossroads turn left to pass the modern kilns and retrace to the car park.

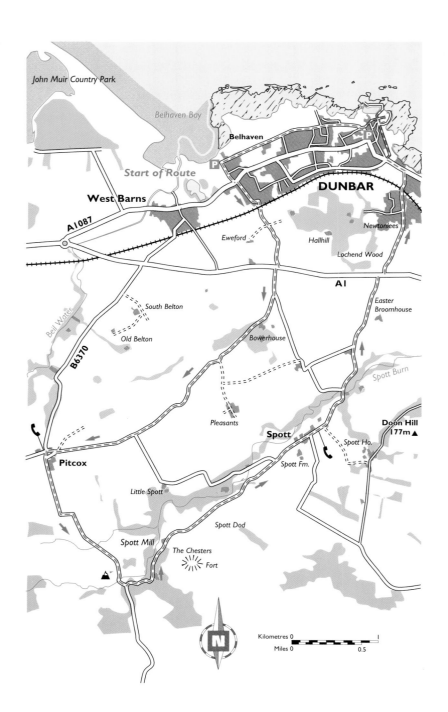

John Muir Country Park

Belhaven Bay

Belhaven

Start of Route

West Barns

DUNBAR

A1087

Eweford

Newtonlees

Hallhill

Lochend Wood

A1

South Belton

Easter
Broomhouse

Old Belton

Bowerhouse

B6370

Bell Water

Spott Burn

Pleasants

Spott

Doon Hill
177m ▲

Spott Ho.

Pitcox

Spott Fm.

Little Spott

Spott Dod

Spott Mill

The Chesters
Fort

Kilometres 0   1
Miles 0   0.5

DUNBAR AND SPOTT

Red sandstone dominates this ride. There are red soils throughout the Lothians and the Borders but Dunbar is reddest of all, according to the historian George Scott-Moncrieff, 'red as the guts of men'.

Leave the car park overlooking Belhaven Bay, set off east-north-east past Winterfield golf links and redness is everywhere: the wall next to the road, some of the dwellings and the splendid clubhouse at the far side of the golf course. You may also be reassured to be wearing your crash helmet when cries of 'Fore' rise from the tee 2 m from the roadside.

When you reach the end of the broad High Street turn left and weave your way down towards the harbour. The fingerpost says 'Harbour', but the truth is there are three. Dunbar was a major fishing town, a whaling centre and the port for East Lothian, principally Haddington. It is worth spending time in the harbour area for much remains. There are always lobster pots to lean the bikes against. The granary is now holiday accommodation; there is a gorgeous hand-operated drawbridge; and it does not take much imagination to picture the whole place teeming with fishing life.

INFORMATION

Distance: 17.8 km (11.1 miles).

Map: OS Landranger, sheet 67.

Start and finish: Belhaven Bay car park, Dunbar.

Terrain: Tarmac. Town lanes, rural roads and byways.

Refreshments: Full range of facilities in Dunbar, nothing elsewhere en route.

Belhaven Bay and Bass Rock.

Victoria Harbour and
Dunbar Castle.

The Victoria Harbour was formed by joining rocky
seaward outcrops and is dominated by the ruined castle.
Mary Queen of Scots visited the castle on three
occasions, which contributed to its ruin. Her first visit
took place in 1566, shortly after Riccio's murder, then a
year later she returned with Bothwell soon after the
murder of Darnley, then finally a further month later on
her way to Carberry Hill. Before she married Bothwell
she gave him the captaincy of Dunbar, which provoked
the government of the day to order the destruction of
the castle. Cromwell is credited with using the stone to
build the quays, but it appears that the Victorians also
recycled castle material for their harbour too.

Weave your way through the old town keeping close to the shore, past the Cromwell Arms, the Volunteer, the old harbour, along Shore Street, Woodbush and eventually up onto Queen's Road near the magnificent red sandstone Parish Church of Dunbar, the most prominent landmark for miles around. There are broken boats, old maltings and all the paraphernalia of a proper port. Even if you wander off course you will have no trouble locating the kirk.

Beyond the church and the old Belle Vue Hotel, which looks as if it is in the process of restoration, there is a signpost for Spott which points you in the right direction. Under the railway and past the little trading estate, where there were partridges wandering across the field right next to the Belhaven Brewery, and up to the A1 road, which must be crossed with care. Another signpost tells you Spott is now only a mile and a quarter distant, but what it does not impart is that it is uphill.

A good excuse to pause is provided by the tablet on the wall at the water filters, installed to commemorate the 'Queen's Diamond Jubilee 1897'. Obviously the Burgh of Dunbar had an excellent water supply well before the turn of the century.

Continue over Doon Bridge at Canongate and through Spott, which is not the most attractive village in the area. There are foundations for a house in what were probably the gardens in the centre of The Square which will destroy the format. On the steepest climb on the side of Spott Dod there were what looked like the remains of a Victorian dump, but it turned out to be more recent: our best find was a fifties milk bottle, so we left it.

The wind had now reached gale proportions and a tanker keeping close to the shore for protection looked as if it would pass to the shoreward of the Bass Rock, but did not and headed bravely out into the North Sea. There are great views of the area around Haddington as you approach the hills of Lothian Edge, but the protection afforded by the glen of Bennet's Burn won the day after a brief pause.

Depth posts give warning of the water level at the little ford beyond Spott Mill, the northern flanks of the Lammermuir Hills providing great flood potential, but most of the year you will not even splash your feet. In case of doubt use the bridge.

Turn right at the T-junction, across Bennet's Burn via a bridge and up the last hill of any consequence. The newly ploughed fields were maroon in the afternoon sun and there was silent rejoicing that the wind was now at our backs. The views jump out and present themselves as you crest the hill, from Dunbar to North Berwick laid out like the map before you. You can even pick out the car park at Belhaven and probably your vehicle. Then there is the descent to Pitcox. Forty-one miles per hour were recorded with the wind, but do not forget that you need to turn right at the farm.

Pitcox is exactly what an East Lothian farm should look like: it has everything including tidy cottages with productive gardens across the road, the 'house' with

Pitcox.

well-tended grounds, a stand of mature Scots pine and an excellent blend of old and new buildings all stemming from efficient and established management. It is a pleasure to ride through.

Several of the fields between Pitcox and Belhaven have no hedge or wall, which give a pleasant open feel to the countryside, and there was the smell of neeps and newly ploughed soil on more than one occasion. Near Bowerhouse, guardian geese stretched their necks in defiance, and it is worth slowing to admire the lodge as you ride past. Care again at the A1, then a final swoop down the wall of Hallhill to the railway and a tight turn immediately under the bridge returns you to Dunbar. If the tide is right you can finish with a paddle in the bay!

The lifeboat rocking in the swell within the stout seaward walls of Victoria Harbour

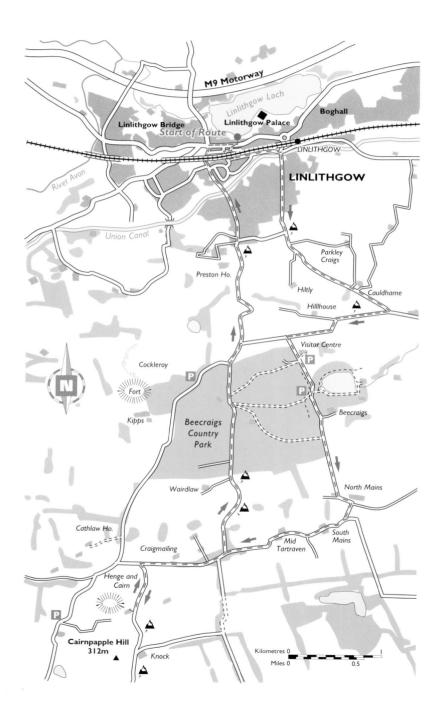

M9 Motorway

Linlithgow Loch

Linlithgow Bridge

Linlithgow Palace

Boghall

Start of Route

LINLITHGOW

LINLITHGOW

River Avon

Union Canal

Parkley Craigs

Preston Ho.

Hiltly

Cauldhame

Hilllhouse

Visitor Centre

Cockleroy

Beecraigs

Fort

Kipps

Beecraigs Country Park

Wairdlaw

North Mains

Cathlaw Ho.

South Mains

Craigmailing

Mid Tartraven

Henge and Cairn

Cairnpapple Hill 312m

Knock

Kilometres 0   1

Miles 0   0.5

BEECRAIGS AND CAIRNPAPPLE HILL

For those not familiar with the Linlithgow area of West Lothian this route will be a total surprise, a tough but staggeringly beautiful ride. Even by Lothian's standards this is a hilly, nay near mountainous tour, but the rewards are enormous. Do not be afraid to walk up the hills: there are views and changes galore. Take your time: do not miss anything. The route has been designed with several options to shorten if the going gets too tough, but persevere, it will only take 10 minutes to get back down into Linlithgow.

Start from the car park by Linlithgow Loch, accessed via Water Yett off the main street. If you can remember to take something for the wildfowl the treat will be even greater. Feeding the birds will get you closer to species one normally only sees flying high overhead; the array is truly staggering, particularly in winter. In fact cycling could well be abandoned for the day and substituted by a walk around the loch; you could learn more about our native wildfowl in an afternoon here than years of study elsewhere. The official information board lists the Common

INFORMATION

Distance: 16.5 km (10.3 miles).

Map: OS Landranger, sheet 65.

Start and finish: Linlithgow Loch car park.

Terrain: Basic route entirely tarmac. Mountain bike required for the ATB Trail, Beecraigs Country Park, which is a mixture of forest roads and technical single track.

Refreshments: Wide range of facilities in Linlithgow. Restaurant at Beecraigs Country Park.

The wildfowl of Linlithgow Loch. An amazing collection.

Sandpiper, Coot, Cormorant, Great Crested Grebe, Little Grebe, Mallard, Moorhen, Mute Swan, Pochard, Reed Bunting, Sedge Warbler, Snipe and Tufted Duck as regulars, with house martins, swallows and swifts as summer visitors and water voles as resident mammals. However, in winter there are always the jackdaws, black-headed gulls, kittiwakes and often the little pink-footed geese. An impressive list.

Linlithgow Palace on a winter afternoon.

The traditional Scottish view is that the Swan, by nature, is a royal creature, none more so than the Linlithgow swans. Apparently they flew away the day Cromwell's Roundheads arrived at Linlithgow Palace and stayed away until the very day Charles II was crowned at Scone. Furthermore, two English birds, which may reasonably be supposed to have other sympathies before travelling north, refused to settle!

On leaving the loch turn right onto the main street then first left into New Well Wynd, which will take you up the first hill to Union Road. Jink right again then left under the railway into Royal Terrace and past the grand houses with elevated views over Linlithgow.

The first major surprise comes when you bear right up Manse Road then right again over a bridge. You actually cross the Union Canal having climbed a considerable height; the magnificence of the waterway engineering is brought home quite forcibly.

Eventually you will reach the junction for the camp site and Beecraigs. Turn right, but it is uphill again! Although the route from here is far from level, by the time you reach the junction above the Visitor Centre the back is broken. It has been a desperate 4.5 km but well worth it.

Beecraigs Country Park is a fantastic development making so much of the countryside readily available for all to see. It is hard to say who will be most impressed: parents or children. There are red deer at the farm and roe deer wild in the forest. You can see the life cycle of trout at the trout farm or partake in a number of outdoor activities. But today we are cyclists. The Visitor Centre is well worth a visit to familiarise yourself with what is available, but especially so if you would like to enjoy the 7 km ATB Trail, which is sited in the south-west of the Park. Collect an instruction leaflet from the Visitor Centre, which will guide you across to Balvormie car park where the ATB Trail commences. There are areas of the Park that are off limits to cyclists, please respect this.

You can of course ride the rest of this route, then do the ATB Trail on the return leg because you pass Balvormie car park, but you'll need a mountain bike, it is a proper off-road course.

Continue downhill from the Visitor Centre past the main car park and entrance to the trout farm, then it is uphill again through an impressive stand of spruce, the road being quite dark at any time. Eventually you clear the trees, crest the hill and there is the relief of freewheeling through open rolling countryside, but it is not quite perfect. Pray for a west wind as you pass North Mains, otherwise the pong off the slurry tank will urge you to a great escape effort!

Follow the signpost west towards Bathgate at South Mains, then straight on past the Balvormie road to Cairnpapple Hill, which is well marked by the transmission mast. This final climb is verging on the alpine with Armco barriers fringing the road. But as you might expect for such an effort, the views are fantastic. It might be worth the extra effort of carrying your bike up the steps and tethering it to a fencepost where you can admire the view, because the temptation to loiter on the summit will be great. Even in winter it is a great place for lunch, if it is not too windy.

Cairnpapple hill-mound and henge, with stone circle in the fore-ground.

Cairnpapple is a monument of national importance. It was the site of a primitive temple as long ago as 2500–2000 BC, and it is thought that the large holes which are arranged in an irregular arc may have been sockets for ritual cremations. Fragments of human bone and a food vessel have been found, but it is thought that by the Early Bronze Age, 1650–1500 BC, the interest shifted to the funerary aspect, and later graves tend to confirm this.

On a clear day the view is fantastic. The flame stacks of Grangemouth are near neighbours; the Forth Bridges seem quite close; and you can see all the way from the Isle of Arran in the west to the Bass Rock in the east with several Highland giants in between. This is a place to loiter.

Retrace to the Balvormie turn, even diving through
the short cut if you've got knobbly tyres, then down an
avenue fringed with deciduous beeches, which provide
an interesting contrast to the mass of conifers, and
back towards Linlithgow in a reasonably straight line.
The mariners among you will be interested to pass the
Racal Systems site as you enter the town, then it really
is downhill all the way to the Black Bitch junction,
and around to the car park. Not an easy day, but one
of the best.

Winter beeches on
Cairnpapple hill.

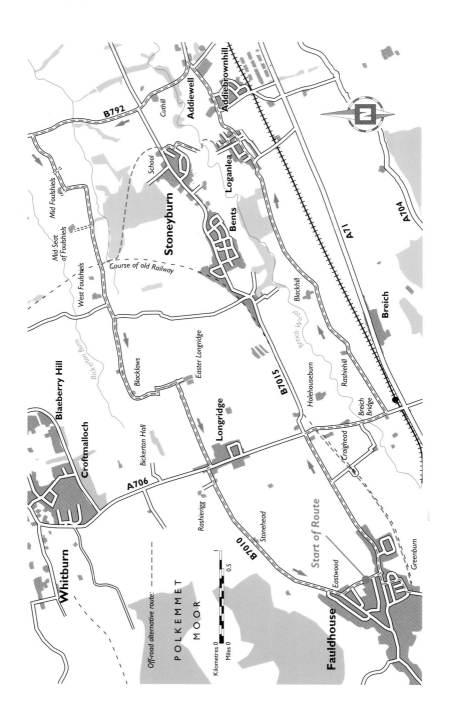

BREICH WATER CIRCUIT

I n stark contrast to the new town and new industries within sight at Livingston, this extreme south-western part of West Lothian has seen the end of its industrial era. The natural resources have been worked out, the little railways closed, and all that remains are the bings, great and small, to remind us of the immense human endeavour that was a regular feature of life in this high and wild corner of the region. This is not a picturesque trip, although on a fine day the elevation naturally provides some impressive vistas, more of a recent industrial archaeological tour. The villages and topographical features remain, but their use has changed immensely.

The Breich Water, which rises around Fauldhouse, is a relatively short tributary of the River Almond. The circuit, which is mostly around the 200 m contour, provides the opportunity for a high ride without monumental hills, but, having said this, it is probably most enjoyable at the height of summer. The reconnaissance ride was done on a snowy day in January when the sun never made an appearance, and certainly would not be recommended for younger members of the family in those conditions.

The grand building of the old school where you start is undergoing renovation; it should look good when it is finished. There is ample parking space in the side street off Eastfield Road. Ride south to Sheephousehill Road, turn left and ride out of town and along to the crossroads at Burnhead if you are doing the strictly road circuit, or right along to the Sheephousehill Store some 90 m away if the off-road alternative is your choice.

Turn left at the store into Bellona Terrace and then either straight down past the garages, or around into Willow Park, where you will find a signpost at the old railway pointing you in the direction of Burnhead. Both options have the same end product. The railway path is a new project, and there is still work to be

INFORMATION

Distance: Road circuit 17.0 km (10.6 miles). Road with off-road alternatives 15.7 km (9.8 miles).

Map: OS Landranger, sheet 65.

Start and finish: Eastfield Road, Fauldhouse.

Terrain: Choice of routes, either all tarmac, or tarmac with railway path alternatives (mountain bike required for railway path alternative).

Refreshments: Pubs in Fauldhouse and Stoneyburn. Picnic recommended.

done. The adventurous will rise to the challenge, which can be quite wet in places, and a mountain bike is absolutely necessary.

The railway runs parallel with the road, at times only 200 m away, but it is amazing how much more wildlife one sees in such places. No doubt much of it is attracted to these locations because of the relative quiet, but there is no traffic to contend with and the rider has spare capacity for observation. Even on a winter's day there were goldfinches, a magpie and Jacob's sheep to be seen.

The Glenburn Kennels
sign near Breich Bridge.

The road circuit in the shape of the A706 is joined a short distance south of the crossroads, but there is only a short distance on the main road down across Breich Bridge past the new Breich Water Wood, the first of the reclamation projects you see, then left towards Loganlea at the boarding kennels' sign well before the traffic lights.

Loganlea is the point of second route choice. The roadies should ride straight through the village, and on through Addiewell to the B792 at the little Schoolhouse Industrial Estate, an interesting change of use. Turn left, straight on through a crossroads then left again at the sign for Longridge some 1.8 km later, back onto a single-lane road. The mountain bikers rejoin another 1.8 km up this road.

The alternative route starts near the eastern end of Loganlea. Turn left into Loganlea Place, which leads to Loganlea Crescent, where you squeeze down the side of the railings in the corner of the estate and follow an interesting path down to the yellow bridge over the Breich Water. You may need to walk this section. Once across the bridge a roughish tarmac road will take you up into Stoneyburn, where you turn right into Cuthill Crescent and around to the primary school.

The real off-road bit wends its way around the back of the school along the old railway through Foulshiels, so turn right at the main road then left immediately beyond the caretaker's house after only 50 m. The reclamation of the old pit heaps has been a joint effort. The work has been done by Lothian Regional Council funded by the Scottish Development Agency, and it seems to be going well. The trees are becoming well established and the area is growing into a popular facility. This could be the ideal place for your picnic in good weather.

The yellow bridge across the Breich water between Loganlee and Stoneyburn.

Some of the path is subject to standing water but alternative, if unofficial, tracks have developed, providing little tests of skill to entertain you. Once again you could get dirty! The navigation is easy: simply follow the old railway track until you reach the tarmac road near Mid Seat Cottage, which is between the Foulshiels Farms.

The routes converge and head west towards Longridge, there are ornamental ducks, geese and what looks like the start of a farming museum at Easter Blacklaws, then an interesting weave through the fields to Longridge.

The final leg uses the B7010 to Fauldhouse through more harsh countryside, past the appropriately named Stonehead Farm and more spoil heaps before turning left into Eastfield Road to finish.

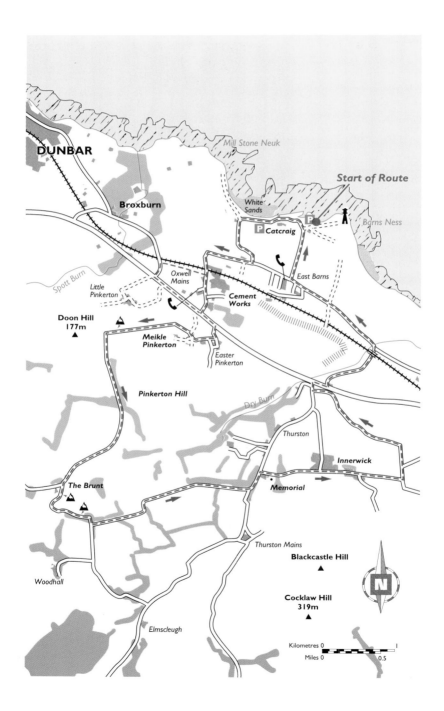

DUNBAR

Mill Stone Neuk

Start of Route

Broxburn

White
Sands

Barns Ness

P Catcraig

Oxwell
Mains

East Barns

Spott Burn

Little
Pinkerton

Cement
Works

Doon Hill
177m

Meikle
Pinkerton

Easter
Pinkerton

Pinkerton Hill

Dry Burn

Thurston

Innerwick

The Brunt

Memorial

Thurston Mains

Woodhall

Blackcastle Hill

Cocklaw Hill
319m

Elmscleugh

N

Kilometres 0   1
Miles 0   0.5

THE PINKERTONS

This is a route of considerable contrasts: coastal interest, the enormous Blue Circle Cement Works at Dunbar Quarry and, inevitably in East Lothian, intensive farming.

Barns Ness Camping Site, developed by East Lothian County Council in conjunction with the Camping Club of Great Britain and Ireland, was the first project to receive a grant under the Countryside (Scotland) Act 1967, and was opened in 1969. It is easy to find: even if there were not any signposts, all you have to do is aim for the lighthouse, which can be seen from miles around.

Whether you leave from the camp site itself or the car park on the lighthouse road, turn right at the Barns Ness facilities sign and follow the coastal track past Cat Craig. The broken surface only lasts about 300 m, but keep close to the shore along the front of the old limekilns. There is a great selection of shoreline bird life working the rocks, even the unusual sight of a flock of curlew on occasions.

Good tarmac arrives immediately beyond the gate at the boundary of Whitesands picnic place, which has some interesting Glenfield & Kennedy standpipes supplying the drinking water. Follow the little tarmac road away from the shore towards the cement works. You cannot miss the chimney!

The first sight of new excavations can be seen before you reach what was the old A1 Great North Road, then when you turn right there may be a close-up of one of the monster dumptrucks at the works depot at the side of the road. Impressive beasts, but greater things lie ahead. The road now turns left towards the main plant at the memorial stone recording the Battle of Dunbar in 1650.

The option to undertake the quarry view extension arrives as soon as you cross the railway. A little path created for the use of the factory employees lies

INFORMATION

Distance: 18.4 km (11.4 miles) ordinary route. 19.7 km (12.2 miles) with quarry view extension.

Map: OS Landranger, sheet 67.

Start and finish: Barns Ness Camping Site.

Terrain: Mostly tarmac, but three well used broken sections, which although not smooth as silk should not cause any problems whatsoever for any but the lightest racing tyres.

Refreshments: None en route. Picnic recommended.

immediately to the south of the railway. It is accessed through the car park and runs along the railway fence. You can either ride along, view the quarry, then ride back, or continue along to the A1087, turn left then left again onto the present A1 road and rejoin the ordinary route after 870 m. Riding back reduces the distance you need to ride on the A1, but there is a good wide margin in any case.

The local rabbits are some of the healthiest in the area, feeding on the nearby turnips, and if you are feeling as fit as them you can always race the 225 as it speeds past! If you choose to ride on and do the extension loop there is another little test: see if you can ride straight up onto the roadside verge at the steps.

Dunbar Cement works and a pollution monitor on Pinkerton hill.

Care at the A1 whichever way you approach and cross at the signpost for Easter Meikle Pinkerton, West Pinkerton and Doon Hill. The road now climbs past the stud at Easter Pinkerton, around Meikle Pinkerton and relentlessly up to Doon Hill. You soon leave the cement works far behind but a reminder of their presence appears in the shape of a pollution monitor, looking a bit like a failed windmill, high on the hill road.

Eventually the road turns sharp left and aims to cross Pinkerton Hill. The surface deteriorates beyond the dip and becomes compacted dirt, but in dry weather this should be fine for skinny tyres. Surprisingly, right on the summit the surface improves again. Stony at first, then, as you leave the wood behind, you will find that the ruts have a tarmac base, broken in places, but tarmac nonetheless.

This is pheasant country. Occasionally there are so many of them that they can be a hazard, flying low out of the dyke backs straight in front of you. So take care, not too fast. It is also woodpigeon country: a flock of at least 200 is often seen in the field beyond Pinkerton Hill Cottage, as you ride down the single-sided road towards The Brunt. Shooting is a popular winter pastime among the farmers of East Lothian. Be prepared to wait or turn back if you are unfortunate to come across a shoot, both in the interests of personal safety and respect for other countryside users. If the estates were not managed with shooting in mind, there probably would not be any pheasants for you to admire.

Turn left towards Innerwick when you reach the proper road again at The Brunt. (If you turn right here, you will end up in Spott, described in Route 3.) Then zoom down the hill to the dry ford. This might be a pleasant place to take a break, by the oddly named Dry Burn. There is also a wildlife reserve managed by the Scottish Wildlife Trust. It might be a good idea to walk the hill away from the burn if you have just eaten; it is quite severe.

Follow the signposts for Innerwick, initially an elevated ride past Whittly Strip and Birky Bog Plantation, then past an interesting memorial between East Lodge and the village. The fountain is dedicated to Queen Victoria's jubilee in 1887, but the tablet to others.

"Beasts" memorial near Innerwick.

> A man of kindness to his beast is kind
> But brutal actions show a brutal mind
> Remember he who made thee made the brute
> Who gave thee speech and reason formed him mute
> He can't complain but God's all seeing eye
> Beholds thy cruelty and hears his cry
> He was designed thy servant not thy drudge
> Remember his creator is thy judge.

Typical East Lothian cottages near Innerwick.

The farm chimney and the church herald Innerwick. When you reach it you find a delightful variety, near jumble of houses: the old toll house, now called Tyme Cottage with both clock and sundial; split-level cottages balanced on the twin ridges of the village; and the old school nestling in the trough. There is a fine selection of names: the Auld Nick, Bethany, Woodside, and, at the far end, Sea View, which is true.

Torness Advanced Gas-cooled Reactor dominates the coast immediately ahead of us, but if you look to the north it is the cement works' chimney that stands out. Head north-west across Corsick Hill and down to the A1 once more. Right towards Berwick upon Tweed then immediately left at an old house, which later became a garage, but now is a ruin, and back to the coast via the old Great North Road. The final lane to Barns Ness undulates pleasantly, propelling you surprisingly quickly to the finish. Was there enough variety?

Opposite:
Barns Ness lighthouse.

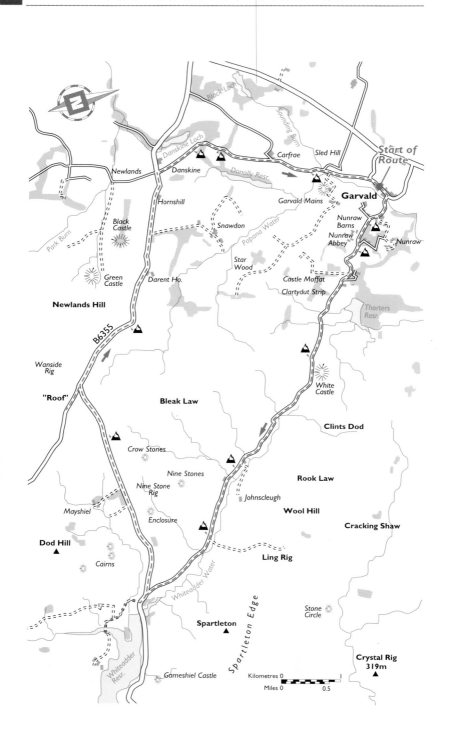

Black Loch

Sounding Burn

Danskine Loch

Newlands

Danskine

Carfrae

Sled Hill

Start of Route

Donolly Resr.

Hornshill

Garvald Mains

Garvald

Black Castle

Snawdon

Papana Water

Nunraw Barns

Park Burn

Nunraw Abbey

Nunraw

Green Castle

Darent Ho.

Star Wood

Castle Moffat

Clartydut Strip

Newlands Hill

Thorters Resr.

B6355

Wanside Rig

White Castle

"Roof"

Bleak Law

Clints Dod

Crow Stones

Nine Stones

Nine Stone Rig

Rook Law

Johnscleugh

Mayshiel

Enclosure

Wool Hill

Cracking Shaw

Dod Hill ▲

Cairns

Whiteadder Water

Ling Rig

Spartleton Edge

Stone Circle

Whiteadder Resr.

Gameshiel Castle

Spartleton ▲

Kilometres 0   1

Miles 0   0.5

Crystal Rig 319m ▲

THE ROOF OF LOTHIAN

Much of Lothian is very hilly, but this route embraces the cream. It is a tough ride up to the highest metalled road in the Lammermuir Hills, 433 m on Wanside Rig.

Garvald is an exceptionally neat village, a tasteful blend of old and new, well kept and well laid out. Even the spaces in the car park are marked by stone, nothing as common as road paint here; one of the gardens even has a brave palm tree, but do not be deceived there is hardly a tree of any sort on the moors that lie ahead, least of all a tropical date.

Depart east-north-east past the Garvald Hotel, around the bend and up the hill towards Priestlaw, which, in case you cannot find it on the map, happens to be the farm on the far side of the Whiteadder Reservoir. The biggest concentration of population in what lies ahead!

There are breaks in the climbing, not many, but they are important in that they give welcome respite. So set a reasonable pace and do not be too proud to get off and walk if the going gets too tough. Pedestrian pace allows you even more time to take in your surroundings, and there is plenty to absorb.

INFORMATION

Distance: 24.7 km (15.4 miles).

Map: OS Landranger, sheet 67.

Start and finish: Garvald Church car park.

Terrain: Exceptionally hilly tarmac.

Refreshments: None en route. Garvald Hotel at start and finish.

Garvald church, adjacent to the car park and play area.

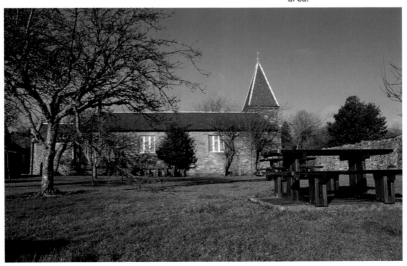

Initially there are holly hedges, very unusual when you consider how slowly holly grows, and straightaway you might think something special lies ahead. Next up is an impressive red-stone lodge at the entrance to Nunraw, then at the top of the hill looking more like a prison than a place of devotion there is one of the most modern monasteries in the land, Sancta Maria Abbey. It is known locally as Nunraw, the only Cistercian monastery in Scotland, founded from the mother house of Rosecrea, in Ireland. The foundation stone was laid in 1954, the monks taking up residence some 15 years later.

The Iron Age fort of Whitecastle with Traprain Law and most of East Lothian spread out before you.

'Fords 2 miles and 3 miles' is the warning at the bottom of the hill beyond the abbey, then you are confronted by castellations on the next climb. This turns out to be Castle Moffat, a farm. The trees on the west side of the road revel in the title of the Clartydut Strip and you may catch a fleeting glimpse of the tiny Thorters Reservoir as you start to climb again. You will definitely catch glimpses of the road ahead as it snakes its way, with ever-increasing severity, towards the Whiteadder watershed, something more akin to the Isle of Skye than Lothian. You may even be struck by a sudden interest in Iron Age forts at White Castle, and who could blame you, but the crest you can see ahead is actually the top, 345 m above sea level.

Storm clouds over
Priestlaw hill.

The concrete milestone at the fort is the first marker on the East Lothian Archeological Motor Trail; you will see at least one more before the day is out.

Once over the watershed you enter a different world. The road undulates, but falls more than it climbs. There are fairly frequent cattle grids, grouse and a splendid elevated ride above the infant Whiteadder. Terrific country. Johnscleugh comes into view, a classic hill farm perched on a knoll above the river, but no water in the fords, nothing short of disappointment. Finally you can see the northern arm of the Whiteadder Reservoir and the causeway creating the lesser loch. This is the place for lunch if it is a bleak day, no matter which way the wind blows you can find shelter, and you will be down there in a trice. The required ride back up the hill is a small price to pay for the protection and probable amusement.

There were gorgeous little tufted duck on the water and an aerial mock battle in the air. Such was the performance of a crow and a buzzard I mused whether the bird of prey had a sense of humour; this one was making a total nuisance of itself and seemed to thoroughly enjoy the pursuit of the crow. Meanwhile on the main sheet of water mallard were bravely paddling and bobbing their way to the protection of the western shore in a stiffening wind, which did not in the least affect the jet fighters that seemed bent on destruction on Priestlaw Hill.

Lunch over, it is back up the little hill and straight on towards Gifford (see Route 12) with the B6355. The wide road at the reservoir becomes a narrow single carriageway as soon as you crest the rise, then it contours gently around the hill, past two more amazing sheds, one of which started life as a large railway goods van, and both of which seem to shelter a family of fleet-footed rabbits. They are backed by Scots pines which have formed their 'umbrella' before reaching their full height; is it a sub species, or is it just a bit bleak up here?

The climbing starts again in earnest at a line of gnarled noble beeches, out of place and adorned with lichen. The hill does not actually go on for ever, it just seems that way; then just as it starts to fall, as inevitably it must, you reach a junction where you must turn left towards Longformacus to reach the roof of Lothian, at least as far as we are concerned. The highest point is only 350 m along the road, 433 m above sea level. There is nothing to mark it, only you will know! A cheeky red grouse seemed to be guardian of the summit; it popped out, cried 'Back, back, back', and it seemed a sensible idea.

In fact better views are afforded on the road towards Gifford, the great bulk of Traprain Law, Bass Rock and some 64 km of the Fife coastline. An ancient sign for the Goblin Ha' Hotel provokes speculation on what it must have been like in years past fighting your way over these tops from the Borders, but now it is down, down, down.

Three kilometres short of Gifford turn right for Garvald at a little crossroads, along between manicured beech hedges, then just when you think you are back in the Lowlands a monumental little hill rears up out of a waterless valley to spoil the enjoyment. But it is the last, Nunraw appears across the fields and you know there is not far to go. The stream zigzags under the road and soon the white houses of Garvald appear. Was it worth it? Of course it was.

Opposite: The B6355 moor road at Kingside Hill.

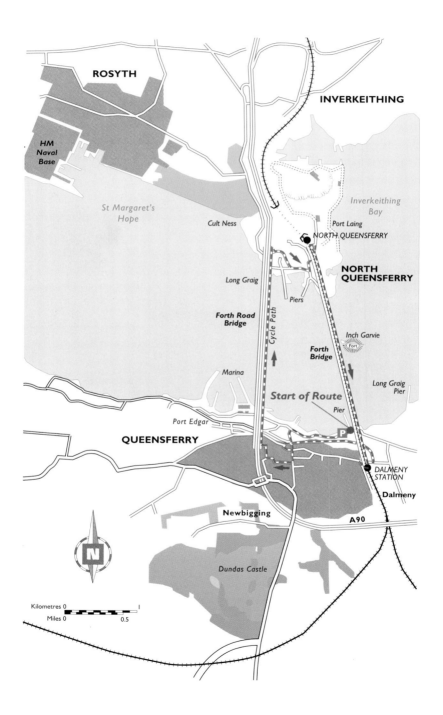

ROSYTH

INVERKEITHING

HM
Naval
Base

St Margaret's
Hope

Inverkeithing
Bay

Cult Ness

Port Laing

NORTH QUEENSFERRY

NORTH
QUEENSFERRY

Long Graig

Piers

Forth Road
Bridge

Cycle Path

Inch Garvie
Fort

Forth
Bridge

Long Graig
Pier

Marina

Start of Route

Pier

Port Edgar

P

QUEENSFERRY

DALMENY
STATION

Dalmeny

Newbigging

A90

N

Dundas Castle

Kilometres 0   1
Miles 0   0.5

THE BRIDGES

The Queensferry Passage has been a River Forth crossing place for thousands of years, mainly because the river narrows here and there is the little island of Inch Garvie half way across, inch coming from the Gaelic for island, *innis*. The passage takes its name from Queen Margaret, wife of the 11th-century Scottish king, Malcolm Canmore. She had chapels and hostels built at both sides of the river for pilgrims, but we take the most modern route.

Start in South Queensferry, at sea level. From here the full grandeur of both bridges is most evident, the Road Bridge an impressive piece of contemporary engineering, but the one that carries the trains is undoubtedly The Bridge. You could be tempted to say that South Queensferry is a shadow of its former self: gone is the shipping, gone are the ferries, gone are the railway workers to a large degree, but the place still reeks of history, still has a unique feel. The ghosts of the master Robert Louis Stevenson, his characters David Balfour, Alan Breck Stewart and Mr Rankeillor linger, as do those of the men who built the bridge, all 4,600. This is a place of real history.

You start in Edinburgh Road near the Hawes Inn and head west along High Street through an ancient burgh whose seafaring past jumps out at you. Narrow closes lead to the water's edge. There are pubs that look as if they should be full of sailors: such as The Ferry Tap, Queensferry Arms, Staghead and Seals Craig hotels. Even the Chinese restaurant, the Yangtze River, has a maritime feel. Times may have changed but South Queensferry certainly knows where it has been.

The hard work begins when you turn left up The Loan, but you need to gain a lot of height to get up onto the Road Bridge. It could be worse, and only lasts a short way before turning right into Viewforth Place, on into Hugh Russell Place, then sneaking past the playing fields and across the car park to join the cycle path near the toll booths. (But cyclists travel free!)

INFORMATION

Distance: 8.1 km (5.0 miles) by bicycle. 3.7 km (2.0 miles) by train.

Map: OS Landranger, sheet 65.

Start and finish: Hawes pier, South Queensferry.

Terrain: Steep tarmac, bridge cycle path, railway path and rail link.

Refreshments: Several hotels, restaurants and snack bars in South Queensferry. Hotels in North Queensferry.

Forth Road Bridge from the administration car park.

The little road leading from the car park through the maintenance area affords great views of both bridges with most of the circular tour laid out before you. Once up here you will get a better impression of the strength of the wind, which is always stronger on the most elevated section of the crossing. Take this into consideration before setting off.

The cycle path is wide and very well surfaced, wide enough to host a village of engineers' caravans and machinery without impeding either pedestrians or cyclists, and the views are fantastic. Using the path on the eastern side not only seems to give you more room to manoeuvre in the prevalent westerly winds but furnishes you with the ultimate opportunity to admire the Rail Bridge. Over a 100 years after its opening it is still a beautiful piece of engineering, a classic. Even if you have never built it with your Meccano set, you will love it.

The view upstream is excellent too: Rosyth Naval Dockyard, usually with an interesting warship or two, the oil refineries and flare stacks of Grangemouth well up river, and Kincardine power station on the Fife side. Before this bridge was built the nearest alternative to the Queensferry crossings was the little bridge at Kincardine. No wonder there was always a long queue for the ferry.

The original light at the old landing, built in 1810. The cross on top is the flue for the fire.

When you reach the Fife end of the bridge several flights of steps will take you down to the main road into North Queensferry. In the days of the ferry this road was the A823, the main road north through Dunfermline thick with traffic; nowadays you can freewheel down into the village virtually unimpeded.

There is lots to see and do. The jetties dominate, the eastern down past the Albert Hotel being the oldest, with Mount Hooly, the ferry service offices, still standing, built in 1810 but now converted into a house. It boasted a waiting room on the first floor, which cannot have held many folk, but without doubt would have provided a great view of the river at the time. The original light to guide the ferries, with its unusual chimney, was built at the same time and still stands. There is an ancient milestone lodged in the wall of the quay with distances 'Edin 11, Perth 33 and Ki' (the rest is illegible). Was it Kirkliston on the south side or Kinross to the north or Kincardine to the west? There is also the modern attraction of Deep Sea World imaginatively sited in the old quarry.

Two rail links round off the tour. The first, courtesy of ScotRail, starts at North Queensferry Station reached by an alarmingly steep road signposted from below the bridge. You may recall the comment earlier that the climb out of South Queensferry could have been worse, well this is it! Try to imagine horse-drawn vehicles climbing this hill, or the early taxis boiling en route to the station, and you can understand them taking the long way around, and dispensing with the services of the spring half way up.

The welcome spring high on the climb to the station.

The short rail journey across The Bridge only takes three minutes so make the most of it (especially as you will be charged to take your bike on board). Again the eastern window could be best, views right down the Firth of Forth to the tanker berth and beyond, and immediately below the concrete artillery battery on Inch Garvie, but do not neglect the Road Bridge upstream.

Leave the train at Dalmeny Station, where you will need to carry your bike across the footbridge, turn right under the railway that carried you south, then 300 m later join the railway path that will return you to South Queensferry. There is a clever little ramp alongside the steps down onto the old trackbed to make wheeling the bike easier. Then it is downhill all the way, high above the terraces of South Queensferry, past an impressive waterfall hiding in a dene on the left and eventually into the supermarket car park. All that remains is to weave back along to the Hawes pier, possibly stopping for refreshment on the way, but if you are a lover of the works of Robert Louis Stevenson there is only one place, the Hawes Inn, and if you ask politely they may even show you a little hiding place in the back where you can leave your bikes in safety.

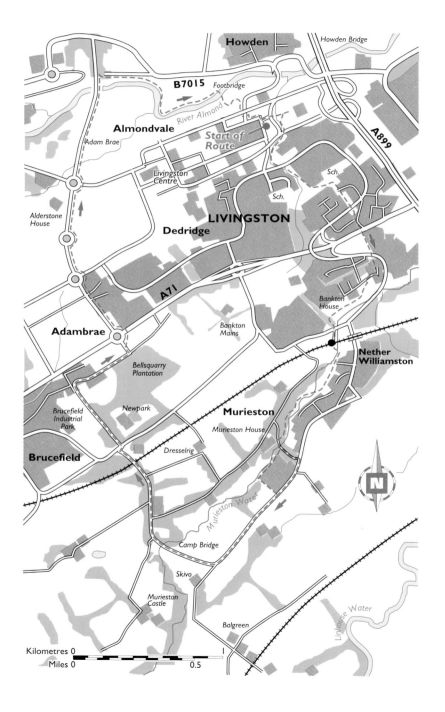

Howden

Howden Bridge

B7015   Footbridge

River Almond

A899

Almondvale

Adam Brae

Start of Route

Livingston Centre

Sch.

Sch.

Alderstone House

LIVINGSTON

Dedridge

A71

Bankton House

Adambrae

Bankton Mains

Nether Williamston

Bellsquarry Plantation

Newpark

Murieston

Murieston House

Brucefield Industrial Park

Dresselrig

Brucefield

Murieston Water

Camp Bridge

Skivo

Murieston Castle

Balgreen

Linhouse Water

N

Kilometres 0 ━━━━━━━━━━ 1
Miles 0 ━━━━━━━━━━ 0.5

LIVINGSTON LOOP

The residents of Livingston will probably wonder why anyone would wish to ride around their town on what, to them, are mundane cycle tracks. But to most folk, who do not live in a new town, it is an interesting experience, a view of the way modern town planning works, and an opportunity to judge for yourself. Something well worth doing. If you arrive by car you may wonder where on earth you are going to ride. That is the big surprise. You will be guided out into the countryside and back again, but in all fairness the navigational instructions are the hardest part of the tour.

Nicknamed the capital of Scotland's 'Silicon Glen', Livingston has seen a Japanese-led growth in its electronics sector, which has set targets for the rest of the United Kingdom. There has been a four-fold increase in both electronics companies and electronics-based jobs in as many years, bringing Livingston to the envied position of having unemployment levels well below the national average.

Designated a new town in 1962, the housing is an interesting mix of traditional and new, the Development Corporation having built about 12,000 homes, the standard of which has prompted thousands of tenants to buy for themselves. You will ride through the newest estates on the fringe of the town and, again, can judge for yourselves. But, of course, it was not always like this.

Livingstone was an old and renowned name long before the famous Glasgow explorer made it a household word. The surname is usually spelt with an *e*, the place name without. The name

INFORMATION

Distance: 11.2 km (7.0 miles).

Map: OS Landranger, sheet 65.

Start and finish: Almondview rooftop car park, Almondvale Centre, Livingston. Best approach by car from A899 dual carriageway, follow signs for Almondvale and aim for Asda.

Terrain: Urban cycle tracks and quiet byways.

Refreshments: Almondvale Centre and Elm Tree Inn, Bellsquarry.

A modern sculpture near the start of the route in the Almondvale Centre.

of the old village on the River Almond is thought to have come from Leving, a Fleming imported by Alexander I. This was the original seat of the Livingstones, Earls of Linlithgow, probably descendants of Leving. More recently, the estate mansion had a very notable botanic garden, and when the house was demolished in 1812 most of the plants were taken to found the Physic Garden in Edinburgh, which eventually became the present world-famous Botanic Gardens.

The river Almond flowing under an impressive viaduct.

Back to the present. Leave the car park by the normal exit, go straight across the roundabout and head towards the Hilton National Hotel. You will see the Burnside Path below you on the right. This is the one you want, so turn right before the Hilton and make your way down.

Turn left onto the Burnside Path proper and follow the signs for Dedridge and Livingston Station South. After 620 m join the Newfarm Path (the paths have nameplates). This time the signpost says Livingston East, then turn right exactly 1 km later onto the Murieston Water Path, which follows, as you might expect, the Murieston Water west. The burn is a lot cleaner; the shopping trolleys have disappeared and there is a countryside feel to the area.

Bear left with the main path 420 m later, following the signposts for Murieston South. Take care on the wooden bridge under the viaduct, especially if damp, then make your way up the vale towards Murieston House, past the play area with the incredible hawser climbing frame and bouncy rabbit! Beyond the play area, fork right across the bridge, then left to stay close to the burn. This will take you to a very minor

T-junction beneath Murieston House, where you turn left and follow the tarmac up to the public road, or stay in the valley for another 350 m and climb the steps on the left. It is easier to stick with the asphalt, but you stand less chance of seeing a woodpecker.

The main road you reach is Murieston Road, turn right and follow it past Skivo Farm, down over the railway, then right and immediately left into Newpark Road. The signpost to follow says 'Bellsquarry'. The Elm Tree Inn stands at the crossroads at Bellsquarry. Turn right despite the 'No Through Road' warning, squeeze through the gates, ride past the Woodland Trust woods, which are really Bellsquarry Plantation, then turn left onto the end of the Waverley Path. There is no sign, but you should know what a cycle path looks like by now!

As soon as you pass under the A71 bear left and use the cycle path next to the main road all the way down to the River Almond, a distance of 2 km. Take care at the road crossings near the roundabouts, pass the sites of the new West Lothian College and Livingston Stadium, then turn right to join the Almond Path North as soon as you cross the river.

Autumn leaves on the track near the start of the route.

This riverside run shows what can be done in the midst of a town, with vision and planning. Then, after about 1 km, cross the river towards Asda again by climbing up onto, then over, one of the spectacular bridges spanning the Almond. This is the Burnside Path again. You can see the start point car park. If you record less than 0.8 km riding there, you have done better than the author. The final access is intricate in the extreme. What do they say about the last mile being the longest?

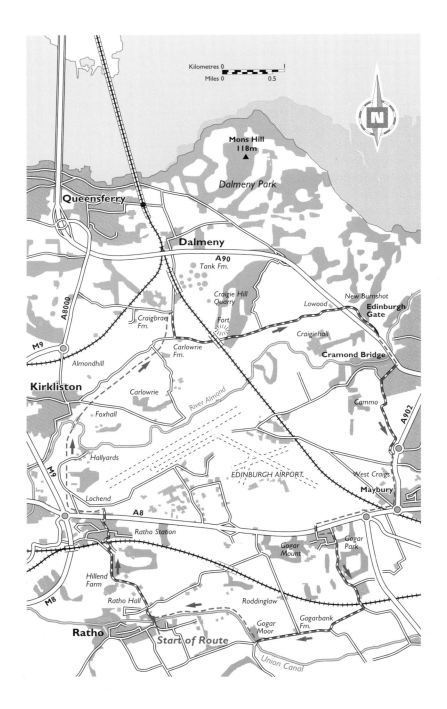

Kilometres 0 — 1
Miles 0 — 0.5

N

Mons Hill
118m ▲

Dalmeny Park

Queensferry

Dalmeny

A90

Tank Fm.

Craigie Hill Quarry

New Burnshot

Lowood

Edinburgh Gate

A8000

Craigbrae Fm.

Fort

Craigiehall

M9

Carlowrie Fm.

Cramond Bridge

Almondhill

River Almond

Kirkliston

Carlowrie

Cammo

A902

Foxhall

Hallyards

EDINBURGH AIRPORT

West Craigs

M9

Maybury

Lochend

A8

Ratho Station

Gogar Mount

Gogar Park

Hillend Farm

M8

Ratho Hall

Roddinglaw

Gogarbank Fm.

Ratho

Start of Route

Gogar Moor

Union Canal

WESTERN FRINGES: AIRPORT PERIMETERS

This route started out as a challenge to circumnavigate Edinburgh Airport by the shortest route, which in reality was never going to be that short, then it was realised that a lot of cycle facilities had already been provided, and finally there was the lure of the Union Canal. The tour took shape as road, rail, a tenuous link to air, and water. It seemed a good idea at the time!

INFORMATION

Distance: 21.9 km (13.6 miles).
Map: OS Landranger, sheet 65.
Start and finish: Ratho Bridge car park.
Terrain: Road, roadside cycle tracks, railway path, canal towpath.
Refreshments: Bridge Inn, Ratho, at start and finish. Cramond Brig Hotel, with gardens, at approximately half distance.

THE WATERWAYS CODE FOR CYCLISTS
Access paths can be steep and slippery – join the towpath with care.
Always give way to other people on the towpath and if necessary warn them of your approach using your cycle bell or hooter. 'Hello' and 'thank you' mean a lot. Be prepared to dismount if the path is busy with pedestrians or anglers. You must dismount and push your cycle where the path narrows, passes through a low bridge or alongside a lock, or if you encounter any other danger.
Ride at a gentle pace, in single file and do not bunch. Never race – remember you have water on one side of you.
Young or inexperienced cyclists should be accompanied.
Watch out when passing moored boats – there may be concealed mooring spikes or ropes across the path.
Take particular care on wet or uneven surfaces, and do not worsen them by skidding.
Never cycle along towpaths in the dark.
Towpaths are not suitable for organised cycling events.
If you encounter a dangerous hazard, please notify the local Waterway Manager.
Please remember you are responsible for your own and others' safety!

Boats on the canal at Ratho.

Following the signs for the Edinburgh Canal Centre from the Newbridge interchange should take you directly to Ratho.

There is a vast car park at the Bridge Inn, Ratho, and another for 'Picnic and Church Users Only' to the north of the bridge. Depart north and follow the road towards Ratho Station. Look for a brace of Mercedes Benz Unimogs at Hillend Farm, the finest production climbing vehicles in the world, incredible to see in action.

The Forth Bridge comes into sight as you crest the rise, but do not get carried away on the descent, you want to turn right onto the cycle path before the railway, signposted Ratho Station. The footbridge you use to cross the busy A8 road can be seen as you cross the

Wildfowl at Ratho.

railway. All that is required is a steady run along Station Road to the footbridge.

If you are lucky you might see aerial action from the elevated viewpoint of the footbridge, then follow the cycle route signs for Kirkliston to what may well be the busiest roundabout in Scotland. It might well come as a surprise to find that a railway once came right through this spot, and even more surprising to find rabbits playing near the interchange.

Within metres the noise of the traffic fades, the old railway is lined with broom, hawthorn and elder, and you are in the countryside. The track runs straight as an arrow to Kirkliston passing the sewerage works on the way. Hope for a breezy day!

Entry to Kirkliston is over the fine bridge across the River Almond, you will probably arrive at five to eight, according to the church clock, and may well be greeted by the pigeons from the loft across the bridge enjoying the sunshine. Ride on into Auldgate, still on the line of the railway, and continue towards Dalmeny. The roar of an outbound airliner could be heard, nothing was seen, but a Search And Rescue Sea King helicopter flew low overhead, the winchman sitting in the open doorway, apparently bound for the Army Headquarters (Scotland) 3 km to the east.

The final few hundred metres of railway path is lined with Scots pines, quite unusual trackside trees, but providing an impressive avenue and regular views across the fields, particularly to the elegant towers of Carlowrie to the east. Drop down off the railway to the right 300 m after the pines finish, then east past the Army HQ (Scotland) and through the cutting at Craigiehill Quarry to the A90 near Edinburgh Gate. Initially you use the old road then a cycle track alongside the dual carriageway down to Cramond Bridge.

It is worth pausing to see the old Cramond Brig Toll, or even diverting down to the old bridge, before continuing towards the city. Take care when turning right into Cammo Road, some 300 m beyond Cramond Bridge, then skirt the Cammo estate passing the impressive tower-shaped folly en route to Maybury.

Use the path all the way to the bypass interchange, where it becomes wider and well signed. Ride all the way west to Gogar where you will find that the footbridge is an enormous ramp, and you can ride all the way up and over the A8 uninterrupted if you are good enough, much to the astonishment of drivers below. You will probably have the easiest passage of all along the dual carriageway. Gogar Station Road will

Canal towpath east of Ratho.

now take you past the hospital, chicken farm and the well-shielded Dalton's scrapyard before turning right at Gogarbank along to Gogar Moor Bridge, where the Union Canal towpath is joined.

Immersion in the countryside is now complete again and the relaxing ride along to Ratho is the final contrast of this multi-faceted tour. A shelduck and a sporting grebe wanted a race, but I declined, choosing instead to roll quietly along at a speed reminiscent of the bygone waterborne transport.

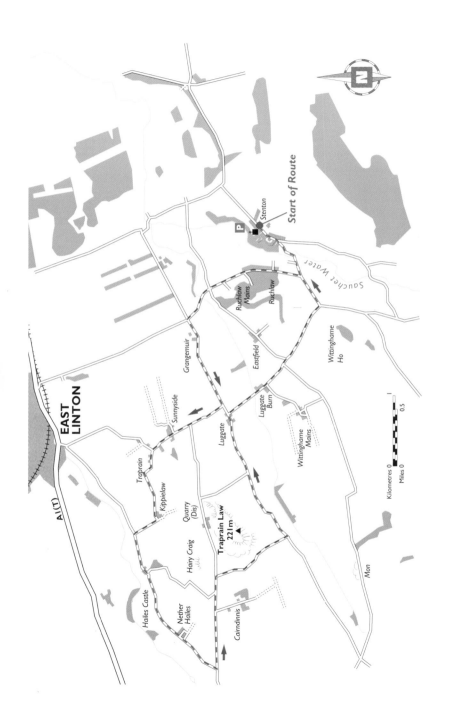

Start of Route

Stenton

P

Sauchet Water

Ruchlaw Mains

Ruchlaw

Eastfield

Wittinghame Ho

Grangemuir

Luggate Burn

Sunnyside

Luggate

Wittinghame Mains

EAST LINTON

Traprain

Kippielaw

Quarry (Dis)

Traprain Law 221m

Mon

A1(T)

Hairy Craig

Hailes Castle

Nether Hailes

Cairndinnis

Kilometres 0   0.5

Miles 0

STENTON AND TRAPRAIN LAW

The great monolith of Traprain Law can be seen throughout much of East Lothian, but in fact it is a laccolith, formed 300 million years ago by volcanic activity. Molten magma was forced upwards causing the surface rocks to swell and then solidify. These were later eroded during periods of glaciation, leaving the Law as an exposed hard rock mound. According to legend a king called Loth, who had his headquarters at Traprain Law, gave his name to Lothian, consequently it is imperative the rock be visited.

You start at Stenton, which despite its proximity to the Great North Road is actually an attractive hill village on the fringe of the Lammermuirs. The Gothic revival parish church is currently undergoing restoration, the project being assisted by Historic Scotland, and well worth it. Before you set off take a walk through the graveyard. The doocot, which now houses about 60 pairs of pigeons, is the tower of the original 16th-century church, and there are many interesting memorials fashioned from the local pinkish stone, notable among which is 'Yoric', nameless now but perhaps a reminder of the days when witches were burned here. It is recorded that in 1659 Bessie Knox and four other Stenton women, who had confessed to witchcraft, were strangled and burned, but the screeching you are likely to hear coming from the verger's cottage is more likely to be that of American buzzards!

Head west through the village past the Tron, ancient weighing scales, down over the Sauchet Water and up an indecently steep hill to turn right towards Ruchlaw on the summit. This part of East Lothian is dissected by many watercourses and little steep hills are a feature of this route. You can always walk up, then freewheel down! The old lairdship of Ruchlaw is now famous for

INFORMATION

Distance: 16.0 km (9.9 miles).

Map: OS Landranger, sheet 67.

Start and finish: Parish Church car park, Stenton.

Terrain: Undulating East Lothian byways.

Refreshments: None en route. Picnic recommended.

Celtic cross memorial, Stenton.

The Tron, Stenton.

its healthy pigs, and in cycling terms for a long hill. There is an interesting new house by the Biel Water, something to occupy your mind on the climb to the crossroads.

The signpost for Luggate also points you towards Traprain Law but you veer north-west past the impressive Sunnyside Farm to visit Hailes Castle first. Splendid engine house chimneys are a feature of East Lothian farms, reminders of the days when the static threshing machines were steam driven, and whilst Sunnyside presents the best facade as you climb the hill, Traprain has the better chimney. Beyond Kippielaw the road plunges down into the Tyne valley, and the thought that all this height must be regained may well cross your mind.

Hailes is one of the oldest stone castles surviving in Scotland. It was probably built by Hugo de Gourlay shortly before 1300, and had more the appearance of an English manor house than a Scottish baronial castle. The Gourlays lost their lands for supporting the English during the Wars of Independence and Sir Adam de Hepburn became the new lord. The castle remained with the Hepburns until 1567, when James Hepburn, fourth Earl of Bothwell and Mary Queen of Scots' third husband, forfeited the lands. With the forfeiture of Bothwell in 1567 the castle passed first to the Stewarts, then to the Setons, but Cromwell's Roundheads are said to have dismantled it in 1650. Unlike many fortifications which were built high on a hill, Hailes is set in a very pleasant situation by the River Tyne, a good place for a break despite the sound of the traffic on the North Road on a still day.

When you reach the junction beyond Nether Hailes you will see you have come the opposite way to a signposted cycle route, but we turn left for Traprain Law. Our route takes an interesting old road, good by mountain-bike standards, which cuts across the col to the west of the Law, but if you are averse to a bit rough stuff carry on below the northern flanks and rejoin at Luggate.

The rough-stuff route has a stony base and quite a few brambles. The gables of an old building are still standing on the col beneath the western slopes. Is it a shepherd's cottage, or perhaps that of a quarry worker? The quarry face, on the north, hosts stock doves and a colony of fulmars, usually sea cliff nesters, but for a bird of the open sea this distance inshore must mean little. The obelisk perched on the hill to the south is dedicated to James Maitland Balfour Esq. of Whittinghame, Major Commandant of the East Lothian Yeomanry Cavalry.

When you are this close to the Law it is easy to understand how its commanding position made it an obvious choice for settlement by ancient communities. By around 1500 BC the Bronze Age population was using it for burial, then a later hill fort was probably the capital of the Votadini tribe, who occupied much of south-east Scotland in the later centuries BC, and who also became allies of the invading Romans. A remarkable hoard of Roman silver was found in 1919.

Traprain Law and the surrounding Lothian countryside from the Balfour obelisk on Blaikie Heugh.

In the latter stages of the descent from the col you will need to make the decision whether to put up with the scratching of the odd bramble or the shaking from the hoof marks in the central strip. It is all good fun, allegedly. Turn left along to Luggate then right towards Whittingehame, note the change in spelling.

The last real climb of the day takes you past the entrance to Whittingehame House and through a long damp tunnel which turns into a narrow sunken road. All that remains is the ride along past sloe hedges and a final flee down that horrendous first hill, which should provide sufficient momentum to take you back up the main street of Stenton.

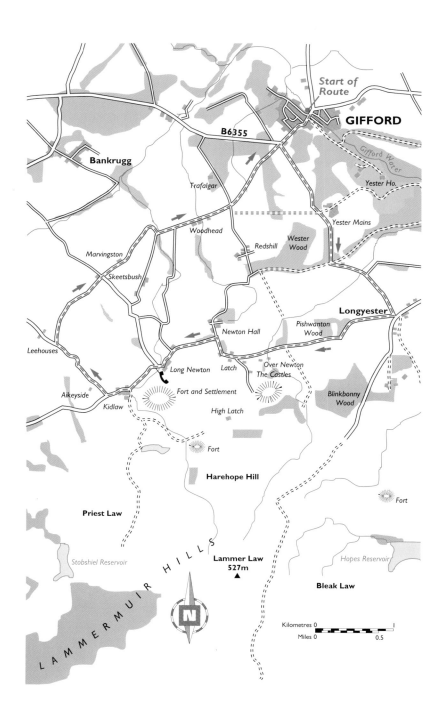

GIFFORD AND THE YESTERS

G ifford transmits a light and airy feel as soon as you arrive. It takes very little sun to light up the main street with its white buildings, shops, hotels and the impressive church. Despite the fact that the original village was demolished early in the 18th century to give the newly aggrandised Yester House more dignified surroundings, this is the largest of the Lothian hill foot villages. Directly opposite the mercat cross you notice The Avenue, which has a neat row of houses on one side and a large green or bleaching ground separating the other line of cottages. The actual avenue is formed by lime trees and leads to Yester House. The main street is the Edinburgh road leading up to the whitewashed church. A J Youngson described the village as having an 'aristocratical air', and you can see what he meant.

Hidden away to the south-east in the woods surrounding Yester House lies the underground Goblin Ha',[1] which also gives its name to one of the hotels. It was built by spirits, so it is said, on the order of Sir Hugo Gifford de Yester. A gypsy acquaintance tells the tale of a New Zealander he took to visit the Ha', whose hair stood on end the moment he attempted to enter.

Depart south-west on the B6355 from Gifford mercat cross, across the bridge over the Gifford Water then turn left towards Longyester at the crossroads by the golf club car park. You return to this junction at the

INFORMATION
Distance: 14.8 km (9.2 miles).
Map: OS Landranger, sheet 66.
Start and finish: Gifford mercat cross.
Terrain: Quiet hill foot roads in cultured countryside.
Refreshments: None en route. Hotels in Gifford cease serving meals prompt at 1400.
Points of interest: Gifford. Hill foot farms. Extensive views to the north (see also Route 7). Proximity of the Lammermuir Hills (see also Route 25).

Heraldic crest on Gifford mercat cross.

[1] GOBLIN HA'. The great estate of Yester has long dominated Gifford, although its present mansion stands at the end of a mile-long driveway which starts at the village. The original castle's ruins stand almost another mile further up the Hopes or Gifford Water, and are now commonly known as the Goblin Ha'. However, most of what remains of the castle is in fact underground. It is fairly common for Scots castles to have a subterranean pit, prison or well-chamber, but this one is unique in having a great vaulted hall, which is reached down 24 steps. It is a gloomy but impressive place. The reasons for the hall's construction are not clear, but inevitably for those days, whether from cause or effect, its builder, Sir Hugo de Gifford, was known as the Wizard and endowed with dread and supernatural qualities, hence the by-name of Hobgoblin or Bo' Hall. He built it in 1267, so may well have been the first of the East Lothian witchcraft practitioners.

end of the ride. Immediately, your eye is drawn to the range of the Lammermuirs stretched out along the horizon, but no fear, you ride up to them not over! This is a tour in hill country but not in the hills themselves.

Gifford.

The well-husbanded estate will not fail to impress, but the little building in the triangular field at Yester Mains might puzzle. It looks like a plate layers hut often seen at the side of a railway, and is obviously now only used by livestock. Could it have been a lambing shed? Beyond the hut you enter a splendid beech avenue, which will be cool in summer, then burst into open country and head for Longyester. The signpost by the burn has lost most of its letters, but you do not need to be a crossword expert to choose the correct direction. It is uphill of course! Strange signposts, or lack of them, are a feature of this run.

Turn right before Longyester Farm, up the last serious hill and then ride parallel to the Lammermuirs. The views open out to the north, the Laws of Traprain and North Berwick, the Hopetoun Monument, Inchkeith Island in the Firth of Forth, the Kingdom of Fife and the Lomond Hills to the north, which had a dusting of snow. A murder of crows may greet you at Pishwanton Wood, then another sustained but reasonable climb

from the Dumbadan Burn alongside the trees of the
The Strip takes you past Over Newton to the red and
white house at West Latch.

There is no signpost at the junction beyond Long
Newton, so bear left at the telephone box and up past
the gorse-covered hillside to Kidlaw, wonderfully
perfumed and awash with colour at certain times of
year. Make what you want of the next old signpost but
turn your back to the Lammermuirs and head for
Leehouses, where unfortunately there is nothing to
point the way apart from noisy geese and manicured
beech hedges.

Unbelievably the signpost at Marvingston crossroads is
in an even greater state of dilapidation. But by this
time you will have established an instinct for the
Gifford direction: straight on and rolling home. The
roll is interrupted at the sharp little hill by Skedsbush
Bridge and then by the most minor of inclines at
Woodhead, which can be surmounted by a judicious
spell of overgearing, but that is definitely the last,
thereafter it is downhill all the way past the golf course
to the first crossroads and onwards into Gifford.

Route passing Kidlaw
farm.

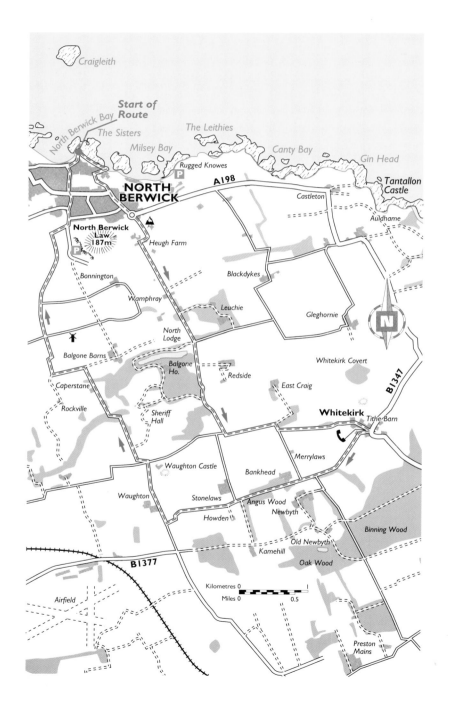

Craigleith

North Berwick Bay

Start of Route

The Sisters

The Leithies

Milsey Bay

Canty Bay

Gin Head

Rugged Knowes

NORTH BERWICK

A198

Castleton

Tantallon Castle

Auldhame

North Berwick Law 187m

Heugh Farm

Bonnington

Blackdykes

Wamphray

Leuchie

Gleghornie

North Lodge

Balgone Barns

Balgone Ho.

Whitekirk Covert

Redside

Caperstane

East Craig

B1347

Rockville

Sheriff Hall

Whitekirk

Tithe Barn

Waughton Castle

Merrylaws

Waughton

Bankhead

Stonelaws

Angus Wood

Howden

Newbyth

Binning Wood

B1377

Kamehill

Old Newbyth

Oak Wood

Kilometres 0   1

Miles 0   0.5

Airfield

Preston Mains

NORTH BERWICK

The first and latter stages of this ride are dominated by North Berwick Law, 187 m, which automatically makes it one of the most prominent landmarks in East Lothian. The climb to the top is rewarded by an incredible panoramic view of the Fife coastline, the Firth of Forth and the Lothians. A memorial plate on the summit guides your eye and helps you to identify all the islands, all the surrounding mountain ranges from the snow-topped Grampians to the Ochil Hills, the Pentlands, Moorfoots and the Lammermuirs. East and West Lomond, across the Firth in Fife, seem very close, but in fact are 38 km away.

Many of the great individual mountains are indicated too: Glas Maol, 100 km to the north; Ben Vorlich, 9 km farther; and Ben Lomond, the most southerly of the Munros, an incredible 121 km to the west, but visibility will need to be first class for that sighting.

Not surprisingly there is evidence of human occupation on the Law from the Iron Age, through the Roman period and possibly to the Middle Ages. There are some historic finds in North Berwick Museum. More recent evidence can still be seen. The old ruin near the summit is the remains of a look-out built in 1803, when Napoleon was threatening to

INFORMATION

Distance: 18.6 km (11.5 miles).

Map: OS Landranger, sheet 66.

Start and finish: Seafront car park, North Berwick.

Terrain: Surprisingly hilly East Lothian byways.

Refreshments: None en route. Full facilities in North Berwick.

Points of interest: Shore life at North Berwick. Whitekirk. North Berwick Law.

North Berwick Law, 197m(613 feet), from the Quadrant, North Berwick.

"Other" traffic near
Waughton.

invade Britain, and there are the famous whale's jaw
bones. The present set were erected in 1936, but the
first were carried to the top in 1709.

North Berwick Law is a good example of the
geological feature known as 'crag and tail', formed by
the movement of an ice sheet which covered this area
during the last Ice Age. The ascent on foot to the
summit will put you atop the crag; the crossing of the
tail commences by bike on the outskirts of North
Berwick topping out at Heugh Farm.

Start at the little car park by the splendid Celtic cross
memorial to Kate Watson and head along the seafront, Melbourne Road, to The Quadrant, where you
are confronted by the classic view of the Law and the
whalebone arch. Climb up past the tennis courts, the
rugby club, then straight on at the roundabout and up
over the 'tail' towards Leuchie. This is a short sharp
shock so early in the ride, but the height gain puts you
into new undulating country, and that is the serious
climbing finished for the outward leg.

Follow your nose past the black balls at Leuchie, and again at North Lodge, where the signs change to Dunbar, but it is still the same road. A hundred metres south of North Lodge three mallard flew out of the wood on the right, then a pair of heron lifted from the tiny stream at the bottom of the hill. Hidden away unseen in the grounds of Balgone House are a couple of large ponds, no doubt the source of good water and food for the birds.

The road turns east towards Whitekirk. The skyline then presents the Lammermuirs, Dunbar cement works and parish church, and the red roofs of Whitekirk itself, which seems to have been hewn out of the solid rock, even some of the cottages have their back gardens in the old quarry. You turn right at the T-junction by the telephone kiosk in the village, but take the time to deviate 40 m along to St Mary's, the historic parish church of Whitekirk and Tyninghame. It is an impressive old building.

Traprain Law, another volcanic outcrop, dominates the view as you ride west towards Waughton. Pheasants wandered idly out into the road at Angus Wood, a hazardous thing to do in front of a downhilling cyclist, but there were no fatalities on either side. Turn north at the junction near Waughton and watch out for other traffic. We encountered a pony and trap! The road now rises stiffly again to crest the ridge near the ruined Waughton Castle, jink left and immediately right, then up again towards North Berwick.

Rocky outcrops in many of the fields underline the nature of the land, but the richness is there for all to see. The ruined windmill above Balgone Barns looks like some giant chimney, then suddenly the Law monopolises the horizon again. Soon you are close enough to see the white triangulation pillar on the top, the Firth of Forth reappears, then the riding is steadily downhill to the outskirts of North Berwick, becoming a hurtle through the streets if you are not careful, levelling out only when you reach the bay. All that remains is to weave your way around to the harbour, a task probably punctuated by a visit to the fish and chip shop.

Opposite: Bass Rock from North Berwick Law.

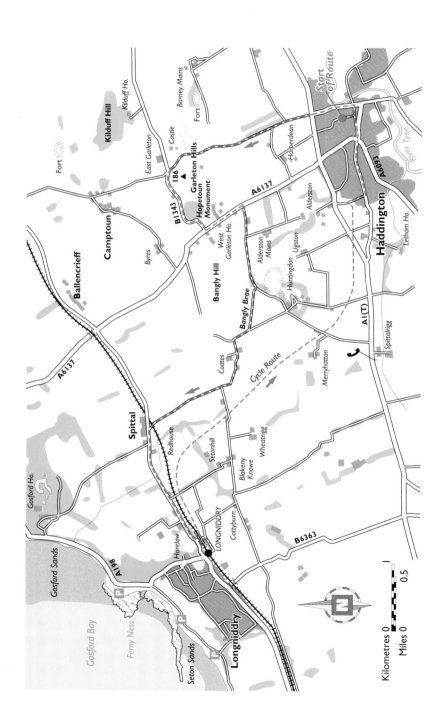

Kilduff Ho.

Kilduff Hill

Barney Mains

Fort

Fort

Start of Route

River Tyne

Castle

East Garleton

Halperdean

A6093

Garleton Hills

186

Alderston

Hopetoun Monument

A6137

Byres

B1343

Camptoun

West Garleton Ho.

Alderston Mains

Ugston

Haddington

Ballencrieff

Bangly Hill

Huntingdon

Letham Ho.

Bangly Brae

A6137

A1(T)

Spittalrigg

Coates

Cycle Route

Merryhatton

Spittal

Redhouse

Setonhill

Wheatrigg

Gosford Ho.

Blakeny Knowe

Longniddry

Harelaw

Cattyburn

B6363

A198

Gosford Sands

Ferny Ness

LONGNIDDRY

Gosford Bay

Seton Sands

Longniddry

Kilometres 0

Miles 0

0.5

HADDINGTON

Haddington is the county town of East Lothian and it is proud of its importance. Many years ago the residents and merchants decided to give the town a facelift, and did so mainly by the use of bright colour-wash, paint, and the renewal of plaster. They were aided to no little degree by the existence of some fine buildings, then much later by the building of the A1 bypass, which removed the roar of traffic. The overall effect is quiet and very pleasing, but it wasn't always so.

Like most Lowland towns in the 13th, 14th and 15th centuries its wooden houses were often burned, but the final burning, in 1598, is reputed to have been caused by domestic carelessness, a clothes-horse too near an open fire. Thereafter, the magistrates decreed that the town crier should give warning of this fire danger on winter nights, the origin of the 'Coal an' Can'le' ceremony. The main goes as follows:

> A' guid man's servants where'er ye be,
> Keep coal an' can'le for charitie!
> Baith in your kitchen an' you ha',
> Keep weel your fires whate'er befa'!
> In bakehouse, brewhouse, barn and byre,
> I warn ye a' keep weel your fire!
> For oftentimes a little spark
> Brings mony hands to meikle wark!
> Ye nourrices that hae bairns to keep,
> See that ye fa' nae o'er sound asleep,
> For losing o' your guid renoun,
> An' banishing o' this barrous toun
> 'Tis, for your sakes that I do cry:
> Tak warning by your neighbour's bye!

Haddington has another potential problem: the River Tyne, which flows through the town. But the same river also powered the mills, the finest remaining example standing at East Linton, 8 km east on the Great North Road. However, you turn your back on the Tyne and head north over

INFORMATION

Distance: 21.8 km (13.5 miles). Short option to Cottyburn saves 5.4 km (3.4 miles).

Map: OS Landranger, sheet 66.

Start and finish: Tesco car park, off Newton Port, Haddington.

Terrain: Tarmac roads and railway path.

Points of interest: Haddington. Hopetoun Monument. Byres Hill.

Hopetoun Monument.

the Garleton Hills, known as Haddington Hill in times gone by.

When you join Market Street turn left along to the traffic lights and left again into Hardgate which used to be the old road to Dunbar, then the port for Haddington. There is an old signpost hidden at the side of the road directing you straight on, across the A1, towards North Berwick. From a cycling point of view, Hardgate could not be better named, because as soon as the A1 is crossed it rears upwards in the most unreasonable fashion gaining more than 100 m in elevation in less than 2 km. Near the summit, the mound on the right hosts a radio mast, that on the left revels in the name Skid Hill, and the Hopetoun Monument, erected in memory of the fourth Earl of Haddington, sits atop the most westerly.

The railway path near Cottyburn.

Having started in the country the view for the next part of the ride is dominated by extensive views of the Firth of Forth and the Fife coast. The relevant arm is missing from the signpost at the crossroads at the foot of Skid Hill, but turn left to pass below the chimney-shaped monument, one of the most prominent landmarks in East Lothian. Beyond Byres Hill turn left towards Haddington for a short distance on the A6137, then weave your way west through the lanes to Coates and Spittal via the high-speed descent of Bangly Brae.

If you wish to use the shorter option, turn left at the little wood on Blakeny Knowe and pick up the cycle track near Cottyburn. This has the added benefit of eliminating the B1377 between Spittal and Longniddry, which can be quite busy on summer weekends.

Redhouse Castle at Spittal is uninspiring, unlike the old concrete grain silos at the farm. They could be demolished at a future date, having seemingly outlived their usefulness, but stranger things have become listed buildings! Turn west along the B1377 past the castle, the recently refurbished cottages at Harelaw, then left at the first blue sign for the railway path near Kiln Garage. Look out for the terracotta boots outside the cottage, than take your time on the cobbles under the railway. They are often damp. By the time you ride past the kennels and onto the old railway you may notice that the distance to Haddington has increased from 4 to 4.5 miles in 200 m, but if you are pushed for time you can always race the trains, at least for the first kilometre.

The railway path swings inland towards Haddington and you are in the depths of the country again within minutes. Unlike most railway paths, which are coaly black, this one is red for most of its length, in keeping

End of the path at Haddington.

with the surrounding countryside. Eventually you become aware of the A1 traffic roar, but this time you go under the bypass and into the outskirts of Haddington, where a brand new Toucan crossing, complete with a special light for bicycles, awaits to guide you safely onto the final stretch of track.

The technique required to negotiate the gate at the official end of the railway path is interesting to say the least, then it is right over the final bridge, down to West Road and back into the town centre.

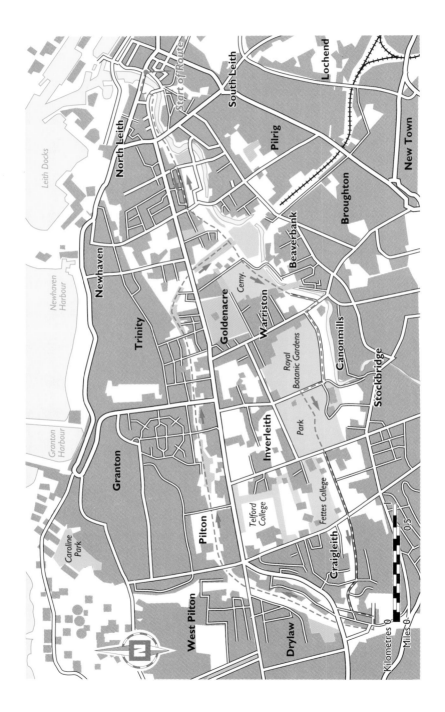

Start of Route

South Leith

Lochend

North Leith

Pilrig

New Town

Leith Docks

Broughton

Beaverbank

Newhaven

Cemy.

Newhaven Harbour

Goldenacre

Warriston

Canonmills

Trinity

Royal Botanic Gardens

Stockbridge

Granton Harbour

Park

Granton

Inverleith

Fettes College

Caroline Park

Pilton

Telford College

Craigleith

West Pilton

Drylaw

Kilometres 0

Miles 0

0.5

LEITH AND INVERLEITH

Think route utilises the defunct railways that served Leith Docks, follows the Water of Leith inland through what was once its most commercial stretch and cuts through some of the best parkland within the city.

Leith is the port for Edinburgh, a very old port with a fascinating international history and some brilliant commercial buildings. Hard to imagine, but this is where the Dutch game of golf took root in Scotland, Leith Links being central to the activities of the game's senior club, the Honourable Company of Edinburgh Golfers, not as you might expect the Royal and Ancient Club of St Andrews. In the 17th century James VI was so concerned at 'the quantitie of gold and silver' going to Holland to pay for golf balls that he prohibited their importation.

Times have changed in Leith, the passing of the rail link for one, but you can still set sail for the Orkneys, Shetlands, Faroes or Iceland on a regular basis. Maurice Lindsay, the poet and historian, advises 'If a man should have to leave Scotland for ever, I would recommend him to sail from the Forth rather than the Clyde: for the lingering loveliness of the Clyde's estuary will tear at his heart strings intolerably, while the Forth quickly opens out its land arms, as if striving to push him and his ship sooner to the ocean.' Dockside Leith always had a wicked reputation, typical of an international seaport, but as the oceanic-related industries have diminished a tasteful whiff of rejuvenation pervades the air, the latest Leith becoming cleaner, less threatening, an interesting place to spend time, but maintaining those foreign flavours, Dutch, French, Scandinavian and Italian.

Start on the bridge at Commercial Wharf, near the floating restaurant Cruise Ship Edinburgh, which I am certain used to be called Ocean Mist, turn your back on the cranes of the new Port of Leith by using 50 m of Commercial Street then turn left into Sandport

INFORMATION

Distance: 12.2 km (7.6 miles).

Map: OS Landranger, sheet 66.

Start and finish: Commercial Wharf, Leith.

Terrain: Asphalted railway path, quiet city streets, but 200 m of busy road.

Refreshments: Cafe, restaurants and pubs in Leith. Ice-cream kiosk outside Royal Botanic Gardens. Ainslie Park Leisure Centre.

Points of interest: Leith dockside. Water of Leith. Royal Botanic Gardens.

Leith docks and the floating restaurant.

Street, head upstream towards the old warehouses and you will see the blue cycleway sign next to the factory units by the inner basin. Keep to the north bank of the Water of Leith, which soon obviously becomes the route of the old railway.

You soon start to pass under the road bridges of North Leith and Chancelot following the signs for Canonmills. It would be an interesting exercise to count the bridges encountered; there are at least 25. One of the grandest for its size is that spanning the path through Warriston cemetery. The pillars at railway height are most impressive. They are also a good marker, because 150 m later you leave the track, on the right, immediately before a substantial bridge which crosses the river, and drop down via the sports field into Warriston Crescent, a fine row of houses.

Inverleith Row, the main road at the end of Warriston Crescent is the busiest road you encounter. If there are younger or less experienced riders in your party use the Pelican crossing to cross the road, then ride the short distance north to Inverleith Terrace, where you turn left.

Young enthusiasts at Chancelot.

This is Canonmills, one time the centre of the Edinburgh milling industry. The valley of the Water of Leith, then called the 'Dean' had many mills, most of them for the grinding of grain, to the use of which growers within a specific area were 'thirled' or legally bound, paying a proportion of the produce for the work done. There were also some 'waulk' mills for the fulling, that is the cleansing and thickening of cloth, for which payment had to be made. These were, therefore, valuable sources of revenue to both the mill proprietors and the city of Edinburgh.

The charter from King Robert in 1329 consigned to Edinburgh the port of Leith with the mills, but these were not further specified. However, in 1423 a retired abbot of Holyrood House set in feu to the burgh of

Edinburgh for five years the 'Canoune Millis' which had been assigned to him in his pension, this old connection being preserved in the place name Canonmills.

Turn right into Arboretum Place, the main access to the Royal Botanic Gardens, some of the finest in the world. They have gradually gravitated to this site over the years but always had a great connection with Leith, no doubt many of the early specimens arriving via the docks. In 1661, Sir Robert Sibbald, one of the founders of the Royal College of Physicians of Edinburgh and the University's first Professor of Medicine, started the Physic Garden on a small piece of ground near Holyrood, growing medicinal herbs. It then moved to a site now occupied by Waverley Station, in 1766 to Leith Walk, and to this present location in the 1820s. It now extends to over 80 acres and is well worth a visit at any time of year.

Turn left at the cycleway sign opposite the main gate into Inverleith Park and follow the main path along a splendid tree-lined avenue, passing more mundane horticultural endeavours in the shape of some great allotments, to East Fettes Avenue. Cross with care into Carrington Road and past the imposing Fettes College. Craigleith Hill Avenue then takes you all the way to Groathill Avenue where you turn left down to the office block, 70 m away, then right onto a railway path again.

This line will take you all the way back to Leith if you bear right after crossing Ferry Road (passing Ainslie Park Leisure Centre on the left), then right again at Chancelot, but there are signposts to guide you and familiar terrain once you reach Stedfastgate. Bear in mind other path users as you ride towards the docks. The path is well surfaced and gently downhill most of the way. It is easy to generate a good pace, and of course there is the lure of gastronomic delights at the far end.

Chancelot, an alternative view of the Edinburgh skyline.

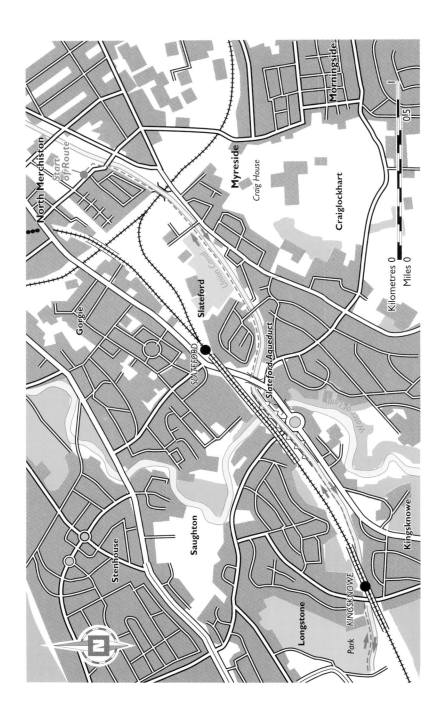

North Merchiston

Start of Route

Myreside

Craig House

Morningside

Craiglockhart

Gorgie

Union Canal

Slateford

SLATEFORD

Slateford Aqueduct

Water of Leith

Kingsknowe

Saughton

Stenhouse

KINGSKNOWE

Longstone

Park

Kilometres 0

Miles 0

0.5

CITY CANAL

This is the ultimate starter route for young and old alike. Parents might have reservations about taking their children along a canal towpath, which by its very nature has water on one side, but be reassured, the condition of the path is good. There is a grass verge between the edge of the riding surface and the water. If you dismount to pass under bridges and walk across the Slateford aqueduct there will be no problem.

Despite the short distance the ride abounds in interest. This is a shared leisure facility in a major way. Obviously you will meet people walking, but you will also see oarsmen from more than one club sculling at quite impressive speeds on the short straights, and fishermen, too, always after the big pike that is alleged to dwell herein. Be considerate and courteous; you will find others, particularly pedestrians, are extremely so. Return the compliment; do not be afraid to dismount.

Harrison Park is the chosen start point. It is possible to begin farther east, near the brewery at Leamington Road, where there is a fascinating lifting bridge, but parking is very limited for those arriving by car. The Edinburgh Canal Society boathouse proudly flaunts a huge Millennium Link banner, no doubt looking forward to the success of the enterprise.

The Millennium Link project hopes to restore the Union and Forth and Clyde Canals to create both an industrial and recreational facility, but ride along here any fine day and you will find that this short stretch is

Union canal at Harrison Park.

INFORMATION

Distance: 6.3 km (3.0 miles).

Map: OS Landranger, sheet 66.

Start and finish: Harrison Park, North Merchiston, Edinburgh.

Terrain: Canal towpath.

Refreshments: None en route. Picnic recommended.

Extensions: Water of Leith ride from Easter Hailes Gate.

THE WATERWAYS CODE FOR CYCLISTS
Access paths can be steep and slippery – join the towpath with care.
Always give way to other people on the towpath and if necessary warn them of your approach using your cycle bell or hooter. 'Hello' and 'thank you' mean a lot.
Be prepared to dismount if the path is busy with pedestrians or anglers. You must dismount and push your cycle where the path narrows, passes through a low bridge or alongside a lock, or if you encounter any other danger.
Ride at a gentle pace, in single file and do not bunch. Never race – remember you have water on one side of you.
Young or inexperienced cyclists should be accompanied.
Watch out when passing moored boats – there may be concealed mooring spikes or ropes across the path.
Take particular care on wet or uneven surfaces, and do not worsen them by skidding.
Never cycle along towpaths in the dark.
Towpaths are not suitable for organised cycling events.
If you encounter a dangerous hazard, please notify the local Waterway Manager.
Please remember you are responsible for your own and others' safety!

already a terrific leisure facility. There are mums and dads with prams, toddlers on bikes and trikes, youngsters of all ages using the towpath as a link both on foot and awheel, the occasional commuter, and all taking place within the city in very pleasant surroundings. Imagine the possibilities when the project succeeds. You will be able to ride from Edinburgh to Glasgow on the flat!

There are bridges both over and under the canal. You experience both within the first kilometre. Some of the underpasses are paved with cobblestones which are less than smooth. Take care. The busy thoroughfare of Slateford Road is crossed when suddenly you are confronted with the magnificent Slateford aqueduct, so impressive when viewed from below, but no less inspiring from up here. The less confident are advised to walk. It is not dangerous in the least, but there is no verge to act as a buffer zone between you and the water, and it is very high. You can look down onto the railway, and down the chimney pots in the builder's yard below. Many years ago, in the depths of a severe winter, it is alleged that an icicle formed all the way from the overflow on the aqueduct to the ground below. It must have been very impressive.

The canal is sandwiched between the railway and Lanark Road beyond the aqueduct and becomes very shallow and virtually choked with reeds. This stretch will take a lot of dredging, but for the time being provides extensive habitat for coots, mallard and moorhen. The bridge after the ruined barge is Easter Hailes Gate, the opportunity to extend the route onto the Water of Leith route to Balerno.

Staying on the towpath will take you under the railway and along to what appears to be the end of the canal at Kingsknowe. However, if you carry your bike up the steps and across the road there is a final stretch, ending at playing fields, before the current canal comes to an end.

The resourceful and competent could weave their way through Wester Hailes and south to Colinton to join the Water of Leith walkway, but this involves negotiating some busy roads. The quiet option is to return the way you came, and possibly ride along to the Viewforth basin and lifting bridge at Leamington Road. Even in the heart of the city a coot had nested near the breweries, right next to an abandoned pizza box. A supreme act of faith.

The splendid Leaminton lift bridge.

The Millennium Link

British Waterways, who manage the canals, will be seeking funding for the Millennium Link from the Millennium Commission, which will be allocating funds 'to assist communities in marking the close of the second millennium and in celebrating the start of the third'. The Commission is looking for ambitious and exciting projects that will both command public support and substantially benefit local communities. The Millennium Link is just such a project. Quite apart from the obvious economic, social and environmental benefits, it will create a national asset in the Lowland canal system, an enduring landmark for visitors and local people alike.

The National Lottery is allocating roughly 30 per cent of net turnover to the National Lottery Distribution Fund. The money will then be granted to 'good causes' in the areas of the arts, sport, national heritage, charity, and the millennium.

The canal, a multi use facility.

The Union Canal, constructed to bring coal to Edinburgh, is 50 km long and was built all on one level, a contour canal, with cuttings, embankments and numerous bridges. British Waterways believe that the potential of the Millennium Link is enormous in terms of job creation, the clean-up of dereliction, and environmental enhancement. This is a project that deserves to succeed.

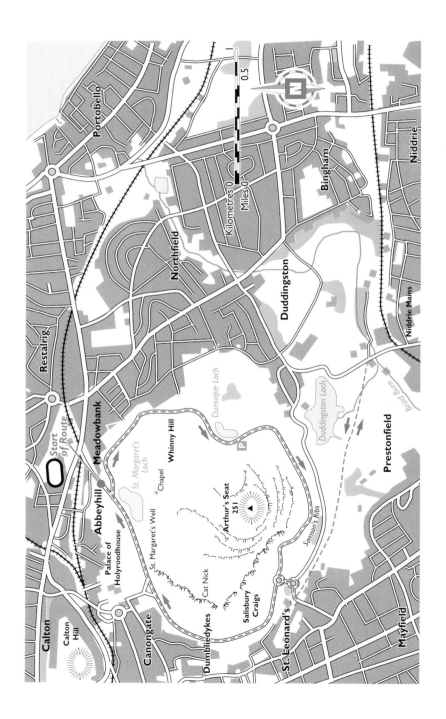

HOLYROOD PARK AND THE INNOCENT RAILWAY

The elevated parts of Holyrood Park dominate Edinburgh, and the line of Salisbury Crags and the huge mound of Arthur's Seat can be seen for miles around. At 251 m the Seat it is less than 1000 feet high but to the north there is nothing higher until you are half way across Fife. A road circumnavigates the hill providing a spectacular tour, and by linking this to the Innocent Railway path you have the ingredients of a very interesting ride.

Start at the car park on Duke's Walk by the diminutive, but highly popular St Margaret's Loch and climb the hill away from Meadowbank towards Dunsapie. It is a one-way system. Particularly pleasant on Sundays when cars are banned from using the road. The ascent is steep and sustained for well over a kilometre, easing only on the approach to Dunsapie Loch, but there is plenty to see and the effort is well worth it. The little loch is a windy spot, but despite this, swans have nested here and many birds use it as a feeding ground. The ride now takes on a truly high

INFORMATION

Distance: 9.0 km (5.6 miles).

Map: OS Landranger, sheet 66.

Start and finish: Duke's Walk car park, Holyrood Park.

Terrain: Park roads and railway path, all tarmac.

Refreshments: None en route, but you are never far away from all the facilities of Edinburgh.

Salisbury Crags.

level and exposed feel, the road being set against rock walls above Samson's Ribs with unimpeded views to the south and west. Way down below you can see the line of the railway path beyond Duddingston Loch.

Serious effort over, the road sweeps down to the roundabout at Salisbury Crags where you turn left then right to St Leonard's.

Salisbury Crags appealed strongly to the 18th-century admirers of the picturesque, but are no less attractive today. The early admirers claimed they were virtually unscalable but modern-day rock climbers find them a great lure, so much so that the Park's Police used to spend a fair bit of energy attempting to discourage them, however, experienced climbers can pursue their sport in the south quarry by permit only, which are issued by Historic Scotland. It is quite hard to imagine that they were once heavily quarried. In the early 19th-century the removal of rock was apparently hardly noticeable but unemployment and severe distress after the Napoleonic Wars led to the creation of a fund to employ out-of-work shawl weavers and others to clear the ground and make a new path at the foot of the crags. This became known as the Radical Road as most of the destitute were, or were believed to be, supporters of the principles of the French Revolution. Unfortunately its creation caused bother for one Scottish aristocrat, Lord Haddington, hereditary Keeper of the King's Park. He had the stone quarried and sold for his own profit, most of it going to the town council. However, when the citizens found out how the Keeper had been keeping the Park, an action was commenced against him, which ended 12 years later when the House of Lords decreed that no more stone was to be quarried, and the crags were saved.

Ride across the bridge into Holyrood Park Road, which is actually the tunnel you are about to use, turn right into East Parkside then right again at the blue cycleway sign through the courtyard of the new housing. You now join the route of one of the earliest British railways, the Edinburgh and Dalkeith, the first railway into Edinburgh. It was constructed between 1827 and 1831 joining St Leonard's and the collieries near Dalhousie. Initially the wagons were pulled by horses, with steam engines to haul the trains up the inclined plane into St Leonard's Depot. The line was built to carry coal and agricultural produce, but a passenger service was soon introduced using open carriages and converted stage coaches, and between 1832 and 1845 it carried 200,000 to 300,000 passengers a year.

The operation became known as the 'Innocent' railway after a reference by Dr Robert Chalmers to the 'innocence of the railway' compared to others which were using total steam power. Inevitably the horses were later replaced by steam locomotives, the line was connected to Edinburgh Waverley, then also extended beyond Dalhousie and eventually to Carlisle to form the Waverley Line. It was closed in 1968.

The tunnel you now enter is 518 m long, 4.6 m high in the centre, paved and permanently illuminated with sodium lights. It is always cool and you are bound to enjoy the run down the slope. However, the return journey up the hill might generate less excitement!

The run to Duddingston has an unmistakable railway feel to it, culminating in the crossing of the tiny cast-iron bridge over the Braid Burn. It was made and erected in 1831 by the Shotts Iron Company for the grand sum of £133. 10s. 0d (£133.50) and is among the earliest surviving examples anywhere in the world.

Entering the St Leonards tunnel.

The ride can be extended to Niddrie or as far as Musselburgh if you wish, but there are busy roads to cross, which are not ideal for the youngest riders.

This route turns around at Duddingston Road, retraces through St Leonard's tunnel to Holyrood Park but turns left to swoop down past the Palace of Holyrood to finish at St Margaret's Loch. The speed limit within the Park also applies to bikes!

ROSEBURN AND CRAMOND

This route, which is 77 per cent totally traffic free, will take you from the west of Edinburgh city centre to the coast at Cramond and back. Utilising mainly old railways for the off-road sections, the ride is surprisingly direct, particularly apparent to car drivers, who are used to the stop–start routine of the rush hour. You will meet a variety of users on the cycle track, ranging from youngsters making their first wheeled journeys to city gents and ladies commuting to business; probably the most smartly dressed cyclists you will ever see.

The Caledonian Railway Company opened the branch line between Slateford and West Granton Harbour in 1861, then another via Davidson's Mains to Barnton in 1894. You make use of the latter first and return on the oldest. In 1981, well after the closure of all the branch lines in the area, Lothian Regional Council decided that they should be acquired and a programme of conversion to cycleway/ footpath routes was undertaken. Bravo!

The disused railways had become almost totally overgrown, so in addition to the necessary preparation of the trackbed to make it ridable, there was the vegetation to contend with. Anyone who has ridden, or attempted to ride, along an old railway that has had the rails and sleepers removed then simply left will appreciate the work that needed to be done, but the planners took advantage of the bushes and trees in many places, using them to break up the long straights and landscape the line.

Initially the cycle track was formed with a compacted layer of old railway ballast, surfaced with fine crushed whin stone, but the facility proved so popular, attracting a much higher level of use than had been anticipated, an asphalt surface has now been added to reduce maintenance costs. This has the added bonus of providing excellent smooth riding. Such is the quality, that there are bumpier stretches on two of the roads

INFORMATION

Distance: 18.8 km (11.7 miles).

Map: OS Landranger, sheet 66.

Start and finish: Site of former Murrayfield Railway Station, Wester Coates Terrace, Edinburgh.

Terrain: Railway path, 90 per cent asphalted, suburban roads, riverside walkway and foreshore promenade.

Refreshments: A variety of facilities in the west end of the city near the start, pub grub and bistro at Cramond.

Water of Leith from the
viaduct over Coltbridge
Avenue.

you use. Only one short stretch, at Davidson's Mains,
remains without tarmac.

Roseburn to Cramond

You can either push your bike up the steep path from
Wester Coates Terrace (the start point of this route)
directly onto the cycle track or ride up from Balbirnie
Place behind the filling station, then head north
towards Cramond.

Almost immediately there is a great view down the
Water of Leith to the Scottish Gallery of Modern Art
from the high viaduct over Coltbridge Avenue. When
the railway was converted for bicycles the original
parapet of this bridge was raised to provide greater
protection for obvious reasons! Some of the overhead
bridges are equally impressive, that at Ravelston Dykes
being one of the finest, and it is interesting to note the

The magnificent road bridge at Ravelston Dykes.

variety of materials used for their construction. Stone, cast iron-riveted girders and a fine assortment of local bricks, the latter favoured by the graffiti artists. Much of the graffiti is merely a mess, but some of it is very well thought out and beautifully executed.

We were reminded of the rural nature of parts of the rail-side habitat by a noisy territorial dispute between a pair of blackbirds and magpies, or could have been a case of attempted pillage?

Graffiti. The young persons' art of the 90's.

The signpost at Craigleith, the former Barnton Railway Junction, has disappeared and the left fork is not too obvious, so watch out for it. Bear left immediately after Sainsbury's Filling Station across the road!

Cramond Brig appears on the signposts near Drylaw; follow them. The short stretch of lumpy trackbed takes you into the Safeway car park, then either walk across Cramond Road South into East Barnton Gardens, or ride along to the roundabout at Main Street post office and turn right. Cycles are exempt from the 'No Through Road' restriction, but bear right with East Barnton Avenue into Barnton Avenue itself. When the splendid houses peter out you join the Spokes Link, a length of track between the golf courses constructed by the volunteers of Spokes, the Lothian Cycling Campaign. Barnton Avenue West then takes you to Whitehouse Road, where you have a choice.

Option 1 is to follow the signs to Cramond Brig where you turn right, downstream with the River Almond, then either turn right again back up onto Whitehouse Road, or be prepared to carry your bike over a rocky belvedere that juts out into the river. There are 71 steps up and 76 down. It is worth it for the interest of the valley, but could become a grind for those needing to assist others! At the far end there are 'No Cycling'

Weir on the river
Almond.

signs and it becomes advisable to climb School Brae, a rough 200 m to Whitehouse Road before using Cramond Glebe Road for the final leg down to the shore.

Option 2 is simply turn right onto Whitehouse Road and follow it all the way to Cramond.

Cramond to Roseburn

The River Almond enters the Firth of Forth at Drum Sands, you turn east and follow Marine Drive along the foreshore all the way to Granton, the huge turquoise gas storage facility acting as a beacon to guide you in. It is always great to ride along the verge of the estuary, particularly if there is a huge tanker ambling up to Grangemouth. Tankers are so impressive when seen from water level.

Opposite the small industrial estate at Granton you turn right onto a path that skirts the gasworks. It looks initially as if it goes through a rubbish dump, but keep as close as you can to the perimeter fence, aim for the rather grand castellated corner piece of the old gas yard, then re-join the railway path at the first bridge you encounter on the edge of the Granton housing estates. All that remains is to keep heading south through Pilton and Drylaw to merge with the outbound path at Craigleith and retrace to Roseburn.

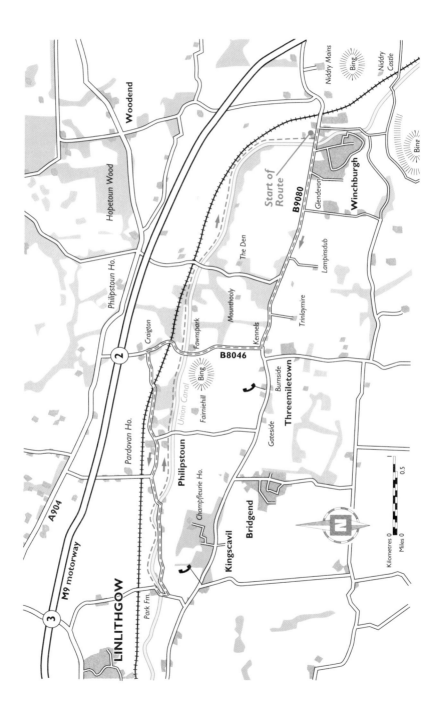

Woodend

Niddry Mains

Bing

Niddry Castle

Hopetoun Wood

Bing

Winchburgh

Start of Route

B9080

Glendevon

The Den

Lampinsdub

Philipstoun Ho.

Craigton

Mounthooly

Trinlaymire

Townspark

Kennels

B8046

Union Canal

Bing

Burnside

Fairniehill

Threemiletown

Pardovan Ho.

Gateside

Philipstoun

Champfleurie Ho.

Bridgend

A904

Kingscavil

LINLITHGOW

M9 motorway

Park Fm.

Kilometres 0

Miles 0

0.5

N

WINCHBURGH

No guide to the Lothians is complete without a tour of the bings, those huge red man-made mountains jammed between the motorways to the west of Edinburgh. These are the monuments to an oil industry little known outside West Lothian, even to the rest of the Lothians.

Winchburgh nestles among them, the Union Canal runs through them; this ride embraces both and demonstrates the amazing beauty hidden away in the midst of this industrial belt. You might think that the name Winchburgh had recent mining connotations derived from the pit-head machinery, not so. The name represents the burgh of Winca, possibly a Viking, and certainly the village was so called in Wallace's time. Just east of the village, Niddrie Castle stands at the foot of one of the bings, a ruin but a fine building, dwarfed by the huge spoil heap behind. Worth a small diversion to see, or take note next time you pass in the train.

The red of the bing shale is a russet red, but has weathered well, elders and rosebay willowherb colonising the lower slopes. These are the Lothians' equivalent of the 'nodding donkeys' of the Texas oil fields. Like most oil, the raw material, in this case shale, came from deep underground, but unlike Texas, the Gulf, or Iraq, this raw product could not be pumped up, it was won by mining in a very similar way to coal. Hence the huge bings.

The oil shales were laid down in water, in the state of a fine precipitate, and are near relatives of the coal measures, which are also present in the Lothians, but the seams were, in general, much thicker. The oil works, at first sight, looked not unlike a colliery, with pit-head winding gear, and often with buildings constructed of a pinkish brick, a by-product of the industry. The shale was brought to the surface in sizable pieces, a few pounds in weight, then processed in huge retorts. The crude oil was produced in the

INFORMATION

Distance: 15.7 km (9.8 miles).

Map: OS Landranger, sheet 65.

Start and finish: Tally Ho Hotel, Winchburgh.

Terrain: Roads, byways and canal towpath, which is in good condition for 98 per cent of the stretch you use.

Refreshments: None en route. Tally Ho Hotel at the start and finish.

THE WATERWAYS CODE FOR CYCLISTS
Access paths can be steep and slippery – join the towpath with care.
Always give way to other people on the towpath and if necessary warn them of your approach using your cycle bell or hooter. 'Hello' and 'thank you' mean a lot.
Be prepared to dismount if the path is busy with pedestrians or anglers. You must dismount and push your cycle where the path narrows, passes through a low bridge or alongside a lock, or if you encounter any other danger.
Ride at a gentle pace, in single file and do not bunch. Never race – remember you have water on one side of you.
Young or inexperienced cyclists should be accompanied.
Watch out when passing moored boats – there may be concealed mooring spikes or ropes across the path.
Take particular care on wet or uneven surfaces, and do not worsen them by skidding.
Never cycle along towpaths in the dark.
Towpaths are not suitable for organised cycling events.
If you encounter a dangerous hazard, please notify the local Waterway Manager.
Please remember you are responsible for your own and others' safety!

Union canal at
Philipstoun. Approaching
the bings.

form of oil vapour, which had to be washed
and condensed, then shipped to the refinery.
It was then blended with other diesel before
being sold.

By-products were ammonia liquor, crude
spirit and gas. The gas went straight back
into the retorts for heating, the ammonia was
treated with sulphuric acid to form sulphate
of ammonia as crystals for use in agriculture,
and the spirit, like the crude oil, went to the
refinery. Further down the distillation chain,
wax was an important by-product, being made into
candles at Broxburn. One claim was that Lothian
candle wax was to be found in wayside shrines all over
Russia until the fall of Rasputin. The residue after
everything had been extracted was beautifully tinted
rocky flakes, the material of the bings, which you will
encounter en route.

From the start point at the Tally Ho Inn at
Winchburgh, depart west on the B9080 towards
Linlithgow. This used to be the main road before the
M9 motorway was built, it still carries ageing trappings
of a trunk route but is now a lot quieter, apart from the
weekday lorries trundling up to the landfill site a
kilometre west of the village. Once these are left
behind, there is a marked drop off in the volume of
traffic, not that it was too heavy in any case. Turn
right onto the B8046 for Philipstoun just before
Threemiletown, presumably so named because of its
distance from Linlithgow Palace. Even by a straight

Bridge 35 at Fawnspark.

modern road it is much nearer
four miles, but this is Scotland!

Turn left at Old Philipstoun for
Philipstoun itself after you pass
the huge bings at Fawnspark, and
follow this byway west roughly
parallel to the canal. The road is
quiet enough but the towpath
seems even more unobtrusive,
and it is. When you reach Park

Farm you can see the access to the Union Canal at the far side, there is even evidence of minor flooding near the cottages before you turn right over the bridge. Once over the bridge simply join the towpath and follow it all the way back to Winchburgh.

The ride back along the canal is great. The wildlife is superb. The whole environment is full of interest and you are so close to it, involved with it. There are herons in the reeds, coots galore making a pretence at secrecy, and resident swans. The first was very friendly and crossed the canal to greet me, but the second, a cob, sitting right at the side of the towpath at the houses of Philipstoun, struck an aggressive posture, probably because his mate was sitting on eggs across the water. All the time the bings draw closer, then as soon as you negotiate the only rough section of the path, which in all fairness is due to improvement, you are literally riding over shale. Stop and admire the colours and the texture. This must be the most attractive waste produced by any process. Some of the colours are truly exquisite.

Beyond the bings the canal takes on more of the feel of cultured parkland than a commercial highway cutting through the midst of an industrial belt; there is lush vegetation, wild woodland and inevitably the bridges of varying sizes and standards acting more as architectural features than practical crossings. As you near Winchburgh the woods diminish and the waterside has an airier sunnier feel, a different character. Do not forget to leave the towpath at the church and retrace to the Tally Ho Inn.

Union canal near Fairniehill Farm.

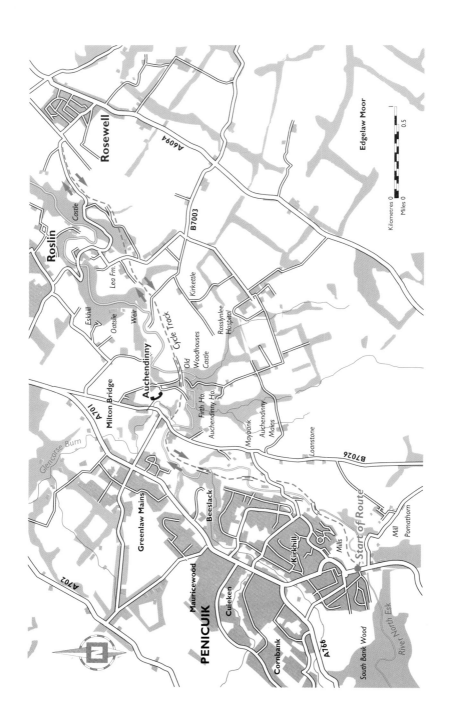

Rosewell

A6094

B7003

Edgelaw Moor

Roslin

Castle

Lea Fm.

Kirkettle

Eskhill

Oatslie

Weir

Cycle Track

Rosslynlee
Hospital

Auchendinny

Old
Woodhouses
Castle

Milton Bridge

A701

Firth Ho.

Auchendinny Ho.

Maybank

Auchendinny
Mains

Loanstone

B7026

Glencorse Burn

Greenlaw Mains

Beeslack

A702

Mauricewood

Culeken

Kirkhill

Mills

Start of Route

Mill

Pomathorn

PENICUIK

Cornbank

A766

South Bank Wood

River North Esk

Kilometres 0

Miles 0

0.5

PENICUIK AND ROSLIN GLEN

From many aspects Penicuik is dominated by the Pentland Hills to the north, but this route follows the River North Esk through a heavily wooded valley, using the track of the old railway built to transport the mill produce to Edinburgh and beyond.

The Lothians abound in legend and Penicuik is no exception. This was the royal hunting ground of Mount Lothian, scene of the tale of Hold and Help. The tale begins not unusually at the Buck Stane, a huge lump of granite at Mortonhall golf course. From here one morning in the reign of King Robert the Bruce, a great concourse of knights and ladies set off to test the boast of Sir William St Clair of Roslin that his hounds, Hold and Help, would catch the white faunch deer which had eluded the King's hounds, and what's more would do it before the stag crossed the March Burn. It would appear that the King had been stung by the fact that Sir William had been ahead of him in the hunt, because not only did Sir William stake his life on the outcome, success would bring the winner the forest of Pentland Moor. Sir William very nearly lost the bet, for the stag got half way across the burn. But Hold got a grip of the stag, and Help turned it back to make an end of it on the bank. The knight's life was saved by the narrowest of margins and the King bestowed on him the entire range of the Pentlands.

Penicuik has been described as a parish of tinkling streams running in shadowed dells, and there is certainly no shortage of water on this journey. The abundance and quality of Penicuik's water supply made it a famous centre of the paper industry. Valleyfield Road, where you start, takes its name from the huge paper mill that stood here; it was one of the oldest of its kind in the country, having been founded in 1709. No doubt there were paper mills in Penicuik long before that, for Edinburgh was then, as it is now, a foremost centre of the printing industry. By 1763 there were three paper mills in or near Penicuik with an annual

INFORMATION

Distance: 12.9 km (8.0 miles) out and back. 14.2 km (8.8 miles) if return by road.

Map: OS Landranger, sheet 66.

Start and finish: Valleyfield Road, Penicuik.

Terrain: Railway path of various surfaces: silk-smooth asphalt to muddy single track.

Refreshments: Olympia cafe, pub grub and Chinese restaurant in Penicuik.

Extensions: This route can be extended by the Dalkeith to Rosewell ride (see Route 21), and still further by the Dalkeith to Musselburgh run (see Route 22).

combined output of 6,400 reams, but by 1773 there were 12, the annual output had reached 100,000 reams, and there were 27 printing works in the capital to feed.

You will need to lift your bike over the huge galvanised gate to start the run, but as you do so you may notice a memorial on the northern edge of the old mill site. This is the Valleyfield Monument, erected in memory of 309 French prisoners who died while interned in the area during the Napoleonic Wars.

The North Esk weaves its way down the glen, the railway inevitably took a much straighter line, and you cross it several times, the first occasion within 100 m of the start. A newly landscaped park with a spring-fed pond, adopted in its very first season by a pair of mallard, leads you to a splendid path alongside the river.

Out of the tunnel into the yard of the Dalmore Paper Mill. Take care.

Sluices and long-defunct mill races are a major feature the length of the ride, as are the many bridges and a couple of tunnels. The tarmac path gives way to a narrow stretch of single track between the river and a huge mill race, but you soon rejoin wide trackbed through Beeslack Woods. Wildlife is plentiful, two of the stars being the Great Spotted Woodpecker and the Grey Squirrel.

The black bowstring bridge then carries you into the first tunnel, incredibly dark even in the middle of the day. It is a good idea to remove dark glasses before entering. The tunnel delivers you into the yard of Dalmore Paper Mill, the last surviving mill on the river, take care to ride between the black and yellow posts that mark the path along the side of the factory yard.

The second subway, the Firth Tunnel, leads you onto the splendid Firth Viaduct, designed by Thomas Bouch, the architect of the ill-fated Tay Bridge, which collapsed one stormy night in 1879. There has been no trouble with this one! If you pause and look back, you will see the remnants of the old Woodhouselee Castle on a rocky outcrop. Only the cellars and parts of the walls still stand.

Work on the path was still an ongoing commitment at the time of writing, a layer of crushed stone being applied to the trackbed to make it an all-weather surface and reduce the amount of

Lea Farm, Roslin Glen.

maintenance required. Until it settles, the climb above Lea Farm will continue to be arduous, but think of the joy on the return journey! You may notice the spelling discrepancies at Rosslyn Castle Station and the village of Roslin. There is further complication on the 1:25,000 Pathfinder maps, which show the name of the castle to be Rosslin. The double s is believed to be the older spelling, a combination of ross, a rocky place or outcrop, and lin or linn, a waterfall.

The railway comes to an end at the Roslin Glen wildlife reserve due to extensive open-cast mining and roadworks. However, a new cycle track has been laid alongside the B7003 which will take you around to Rosewell, and will link up with another section which will take you to Dalkeith in due course.

It was intended to make this a circular tour, returning to Penicuik by lesser roads and byways, but this is not recommended for young or inexperienced cyclists. It is necessary to use either the B7026 or the A701, both of which carry a lot of motor traffic at certain times of day, so the favoured option is to return the way you came. You will see just as much on the way back.

Ongoing work on the path near Rosslyn Castle Station.

If you choose to return by road you will pass the site of Roslin Mills, the biggest gunpowder mill in the country, at least until it closed, due to mining subsidence in 1954. It supplied munitions for the Napoleonic, First and Second World Wars as well as explosives for the mining and quarrying industries. Carved on the face of a rock within the site is 1815, a record of the fact that Roslin powder was used at Waterloo. The black powder had long ceased to be used for guns before the mill closed, but it remained popular with quarrymen, who liked it for its 'gentle, heaving action'.

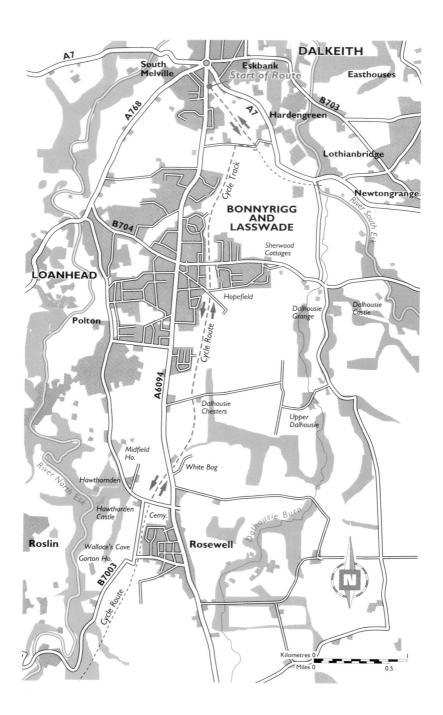

DALKEITH TO ROSEWELL

I f you follow the road south-west from Dalkeith towards Rosewell you soon become aware of the change from sheltered, comfortable stability to a more stark, raw region, even on a nice day. Despite good farming land the area looks wide open, verging on the bleak. This impression is also conveyed from the railway, regardless of the proximity of new housing.

Many of the old walls have cracked and crumbled, a legacy of the extensive mining industry centred on Dalhousie, the railway you use terminating at St Leonard's on the edge of Holyrood Park in Edinburgh (see Route 17), and built specifically to carry this coal to the capital. The mines are gone, the fields are green again, but the district still has that unmistakable pit village feel to it for anyone who ever had mining connections.

This is not the prettiest ride in the book, but there is lots to see and it serves three purposes. It is a safe traffic-free route in an area where even the side roads carry a fair volume of traffic; it is a good learning run;

INFORMATION

Distance: 10.7 km (6.6 miles).

Map: OS Landranger, sheet 66.

Start and finish: Lasswade Road, Eskbank, Dalkeith.

Terrain: Railway path of various surfaces: asphalt to compacted mud.

Refreshments: None en route. Picnic recommended

Extensions: Roslin to Penicuik to the south-west (see Route 20). Dalkeith to Musselburgh to the north-east (see Route 22).

The railway path at Hardengreen farm

The infilled bridge at Hardengreen farm, distant Moorfoot Hills on the horizon.

and it provides a link between Roslin and Dalkeith enabling the most adventurous rider to complete the ride from Penicuik to the coast.

The route starts at the present end of the path off Lasswade Road, Eskbank, accessed opposite a garage and accident repair shop. Look over the side down into the railway cutting and you will appreciate what an excellent job the local authority has done in creating the path from the old railway, the untamed section providing ample evidence of their efforts. Look also at the fence along the top of the embankment, surely boasting the most substantial fenceposts in the Lothians: railway sleepers!

The long slope down to the trackbed is a great start, then it is along through newly planted birches, which always do well in this sort of environment, and up through the old sawmill site to Hardengreen Farm. There is very little trace of the railway that went to Newtongrange and beyond, but if you pause at the bridge, now infilled, and look towards the Moorfoot Hills, the line can still be discerned.

Turn right, away from the farm, along a bumpy lane then left at the bottom to cross the magnificent new footbridge which spans the A7 trunk road. This now leads you past Lasswade, still on excellent tarmac, through a small new housing development astride the old railway, to Dundas Street, the B704. Take care crossing the road, which can be quite busy at certain times of day, and continue to follow the course of the railway. The old platforms have been retained and landscaped to great effect, but the asphalt comes to an abrupt end in another 300 m.

The line is still quite obvious along the back of the houses, but as yet has not been improved in any way. It is perfectly ridable and well used, but demands a little more bike control, sensible gear selection and appreciation of the terrain. A short but interesting

On the outskirts of Lasswade.

stretch from a bike-handling point of view, which is all valuable experience because it is downhill on the way back and you will probably be going a bit quicker. The surface improves well before you reach Dalhousie Chesters and thereafter is undergoing considerable refurbishment with the application of a layer of crushed stone.

The route terminates at Rosewell cemetery for the time being, due to extensive open-cast mining and ancillary works. There are remnants of the old line skirting the north-western side of Rosewell, and a link under construction to Roslin Glen that will extend the traffic-free riding possibilities to the south-west, but for the time being the sensible option is to return by your outward route. After all it is downhill all the way.

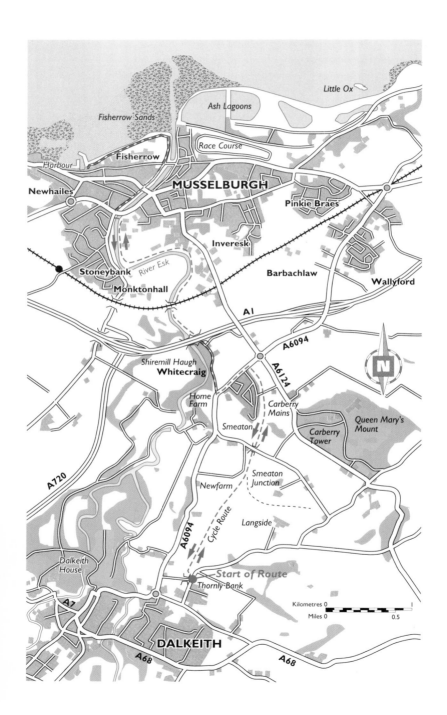

DALKEITH TO MUSSELBURGH

Lothian Regional Council must be complimented on their efforts to create traffic-free cycling facilities, and this route is one of the very best. The first kilometre and a half is smooth tarmac, then there is a stretch of original railway line to Whitecraig, the third section is the excellent riverside path alongside the Esk, then finally the shared facility to the mouth of the river, where you could terminate the journey, or ride along the promenade to Fisherrow, as described here.

Originally it was intended to ride a circular route, but once the rail and riverside run from Dalkeith to Musselburgh had been covered, it was felt that it could not be bettered, both from a scenic and safety point of view. It therefore stands as an out and back ride.

The ride starts at the eastern end of the trading estate at Thorny Bank, Dalkeith, on immaculate asphalt, a signpost points you in the direction of Musselburgh. Within a few hundred metres of the start you get a glimpse of the sea. This can either act as great encouragement or a deterrent, an opportunity to ride from the depths of the countryside to the coast, or gasps when you realise that it will be uphill all the way back. Do not despair, the reality is much gentler than appears at first, the initial part of the return journey is flat, alongside the River Esk, and apart from a single-100 m burst onto the road from the riverside path at Shiremill Haugh, the climbing is all done on the old railway track, and consequently on very gentle gradients.

New birchwood strikes you as you pass beneath the pylons at Smeaton Junction, the differing levels of the tracks still evident. There is a signpost indicating the possible connection to Ormiston on the Pencaitland railway path (see Route 1), then a change of surface. The pristine tarmac gives way to the original trackbed, still smooth but narrow and entertainingly loose, a typical

INFORMATION

Distance: 18.8 km (11.6 miles).

Map: OS Landranger, sheet 66.

Start and finish: Thorny Bank, Dalkeith.

Terrain: Railway path: asphalted and untreated, tarmac streets and good compacted riverside path.

Refreshments: Full facilities in Musselburgh. Only slightly less at Fisherrow Harbour.

Extensions: This route could be started at Fisherrow, on the coast, and extended inland as far as Penicuik using the Dalkeith to Rosewell (see Route 21) and Penicuik to Roslin Glen rides (see Route 20).

Change of surface at Smeaton Junction.

miners' thoroughfare. When dry, the loosest material collects in the deepest central part of the path, which can make the riding a little heavier or disconcert novices, but there is nothing to fear, the apparent looseness is easily overcome by continuing to pedal firmly or simply riding on the outer edge, where it will still be compacted and firm. When wet, of course, this stretch will sprinkle you black!

New trees, many of them early spring flowerers, are a pleasant feature of the embankment around Whitecraig, but when you reach the end, near the Dolphin Inn, divert off the right-hand side via a broken path to the road. It is still possible for the skilled to ride off the end, down what was the old bridge abutment, but the wild dog roses are growing vigorously and will scratch you to death. You have been warned!

Cycle route alongside the River Esk near Wedderburn House, Inveresk.

It is necessary to use 500 m of the A6094 through Whitecraig. Turn left at the Dolphin Inn, where you will see a blue cycle route sign, ride to the far end of the village and turn right into Cowpits Road, just beyond St John's Church, where another blue signpost, this time announcing the River Esk Walkway, tells you that Musselburgh is some two and a half miles distant. You are then virtually traffic free again. Bear slightly left, down under the A1 Great North Road at the first right-hand bend to join the riverside path. The surface in the underpass is large chippings, which might prove disconcerting. You enter a new world down by the river, lush vegetation, dappled shade and a great variety of waterside wildlife. Take note of the sandy soil on the banks: a sure sign of inundation from time to time, but an ideal medium for wild garlic, which you may well smell before seeing. This is another route well worth revisiting at a different time of year to see the changes.

The riverside path ends at the Inveresk Industrial Estate. Look to cross the river by the footbridge before you reach the main road, then turn right into Eskview Terrace and hug the north bank of the river as closely as possible using quiet side streets all the way to New Street, where the riverside path becomes the preserve of cyclists and pedestrians once again. Swans now dominate the wildlife scene, some even nesting close to the boundary fence of the side streets, another pair claiming a mid-river island. They appear little disturbed by human presence, but please do not abuse their trust, or push your luck: you may become subject to attack!

You can terminate your journey on reaching Fisherrow Sands at the mouth of the river, or ride along the promenade to Fisherrow Harbour, where food is available and there is often a deal of marine activity to interest the spectator.

Fisherrow, although now joined by building to Musselburgh, was a quite distinct community. Self contained, it had its own traditions and way of life, linked closely to the fishing industry. There were never a great many boats actually based at Fisherrow, but smacks came in here from all along the Fife coast to land their fish for the Edinburgh market. It was the fishwives who made the community distinctive, usually carrying the fish on their backs, often for great distances in their great osier creels, no doubt made from local willow harvested

Harbour Office, Fisherrow.

from the very trees you passed on your ride down the Esk. If the boats came in late, the catches would be speeded to Edinburgh by relay deliveries, and the 8 km to market done in three-quarters of an hour. There is a case on record of three of the fishwives carrying a heavy load of herring from Dunbar to Edinburgh, a distance of 46.8 km, in five hours!

Replete with the delicacies of Fisherrow, your return ride should be just as interesting. The gradients are easy, and even if the legs tire in the final stages the sleek asphalt will aid your glide to the finish.

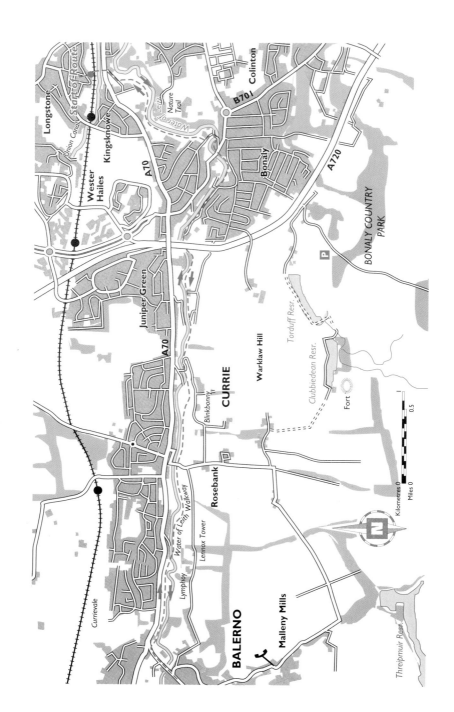

Longstone

Start of Route

Union Canal

Kingsknowe

Wester Hailes

A70

Water of Leith Nature Trail

Colinton

B701

Bonaly

A720

BONALY COUNTRY PARK

P

Juniper Green

Torduff Resr.

Clubbiedean Resr.

Warklaw Hill

CURRIE

Blinkbonny

Fort

Rosebank

A70

Water of Leith Walkway

Lymphoy

Lennox Tower

Curriervale

BALERNO

Malleny Mills

Threipmuir Resr.

N

Kilometres 0
Miles 0
0.5

WATER OF LEITH

The true start of this ride is the Union Canal Bridge at Easter Hailes Gate, by Lanark Road. It then follows the route of the old railway south-west to Balerno. An alternative beginning is the car park at the site of the old Colinton Station by the Water of Leith, which you will pass through in any case if riding the full tour.

Union Canal bridge at Easter Hailes Gate.

The Caledonian Railway Company built this line in 1874 to carry goods to and from the mills on the river because access by road was difficult due to the steep valley sides. This is still a factor; the few roads servicing the district are always busy, so this is an out and back route on a facility that is as safe as it is entertaining.

There were over 70 mills using the Water of Leith as their power source in its heyday, which made it one of the busiest industrial rivers in Scotland. The mills produced flour, paper, spices, snuff, anything that needed grinding or crushing, and cloth nearer the sea at Leith. The world-famous Scotts Porage Oats were made at the mill in Colinton from 1909 to 1947.

There is only one tunnel on the line, Colinton, which you pass through before reaching the site of the old station. It is still dark, damp and gloomy. Remove any shades before entering, otherwise you will not see where you are going and use your lights if necessary. (The line finally closed in 1967.)

INFORMATION

Distance: 15.5 km (9.6 miles). 12.2 km (7.6 miles) if starting from Colinton Station.

Map: OS Landranger, sheet 66.

Start and finish: Union Canal Bridge, Easter Hailes Gate, by Lanark Road, Kingsknowe, Edinburgh. Or car park, site of Colinton Station.

Terrain: Railway path, then a short stretch of public road into Balerno.

Refreshments: Soup and snacks at the Upper Crust Delicatessen, the Malleny Arms or Grey Horse, Balerno. Delicatessen closed Sundays, but open throughout the winter.

Extensions: This route can be used as an extension of the City Canal ride (see Route 16) and curtailed as riders wish simply by turning around at any point. The other potential extension is the Balerno Loop (see Route 24), which is a more serious undertaking, because it is both hilly and entirely upon public roads.

Colinton has long been swallowed up by the city, but was regarded as the last of the Pentland villages clinging to the river and always a favoured stronghold of professionals from Edinburgh. Even before the railway was built many residents travelled into the city by coach on a daily basis, but there was little commerce as such. In those days almost the only trace of commerce was the tomb in the kirk of James Gillespie, founder of the school of that name, who made his money from the snuff ground in great quantities by the Water of Leith. A tobacconist from the High Street, he was one of the worthiest men in Colinton, but in his day had to suffer many a jibe, such as Henry Erskine's remark when he saw Gillespie in his first coach:

Autumn leaves add a touch of colour.

> Wha wad ha' thocht it
> That noses had bocht it?

The real Colinton is the village by the river, on a particularly choice stretch where the valley widens to an amphitheatre, which collects the sun's warmth on a summer evening, with the river and the railway winding above it on the shady side. The woods are still as dense as ever: cool in summer, ablaze with colour in autumn and compact enough to dull the winter's wind. This is a ride well worth doing at any time of the year.

Robert Louis Stevenson's grandfather, the Reverend Lewis Balfour was minister at Colinton and R.L.S. spent much time down by the river. 'That dirty Water of Leith' he called it, but remembered every bend and eddy. There were and still are the weirs, where the water lies 'deep and darkling'. In those days the weirs received the contents of the mill-lades, which caused the 'curded froth of many other mills' to hover on the surface. In the dark, dense woods R.L.S. recalls 'the smell of water rising from all around, with the added tang of paper mills, the sound of water everywhere, and the sound of mills – the wheel and the dam singing their alternate strain, the birds on every bush and from every corner of the overhanging woods pealing out their notes until the air throbbed with them'. Is it too much to expect that the ghost of the greatest story-teller still treads these paths and heughs occasionally?

The path itself is easy to follow: it crosses the river a couple of times via the old railway bridges. There is more than one place where a wrong route choice can take you into a derelict mill site, but these are minor impediments and not without interest. The general rule is take the high road: you can always save the lower alternatives for the return journey. When you encounter a tarmac road, as you will, always look to re-join the riverside path as quickly as possible.

There are many mill-races and sluices still remaining, some very close to the track, seemingly stuck to the embankment, their brickwork the haunt of dippers and wagtails. You ride, virtually unnoticed, beneath the city bypass, then past the only surviving corn mill, that of Alexander Inglis & Co., powered as you might expect by electricity, but grinding corn from as far away as Northumberland.

Main Street in Balerno.

Juniper Green and Currie, where the great mountaineer Dougal Haston honed his strength and skills on the railway stonework, are passed by and you arrive quite suddenly at Balerno. The old main street has been pedestrianised and there is a small paved square where you may dine al fresco. On the other hand you may prefer to choose a quieter place by the river.

You may expect the return journey to be quicker because it is mainly downhill, but do not rush it: this is a tour to be enjoyed at leisure.

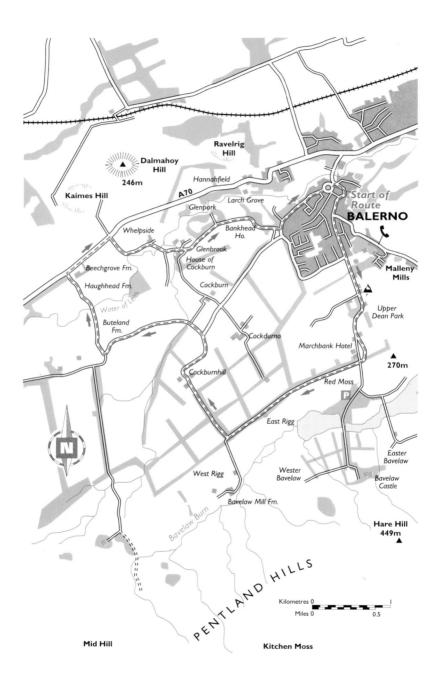

Ravelrig
Hill

Dalmahoy
Hill
246m

Kaimes Hill

Hannahfield

A70

Larch Grove

*Start of
Route*
BALERNO

Glenpark

Whelpside

Bankhead
Ho.

Glenbrook

House of
Cockburn

**Malleny
Mills**

Beechgrove Fm.

Cockburn

Haughhead Fm.

Water of Leith

Upper
Dean Park

Buteland
Fm.

Cockdurno

Marchbank Hotel

270m

Cockburnhill

Red Moss

P

East Rigg

Easter
Bavelaw

West Rigg

Wester
Bavelaw

Bavelaw
Castle

Bavelaw Mill Fm.

Bavelaw Burn

Hare Hill
449m

P E N T L A N D   H I L L S

Kilometres 0 ——————— 1
Miles 0 ——————— 0.5

Mid Hill

Kitchen Moss

BALERNO LOOP

Balerno was the end of the Caledonian Railway branch line along the Water of Leith, an ideal launching pad for the many walkers bent on a day in the Pentland Hills in the first half of the 20th century. It is thought that Winston Churchill may have been the last passenger to board a train from Balerno, his official train having used the line on a visit to Edinburgh.

The name of the village itself has a distinct foreign flavour, Italian or even Irish? There has been no conclusive explanation, but where else could you ride from suburban comfort to really wild moor and mountain in 20 minutes? A fact most forcibly driven home in winter. Or contemplate even greater diversity when you consider a fit cyclist can ride from Princes Street to this part of the Pentlands in less than an hour. Is any major city in the world so well situated?

There was a great paper mill at Balerno; sadly only the office entrance still stands. The smell of the Spanish esparto grass, the principal raw material in making of its fine papers, is long gone. Even after the railway closed the mill worked on; there were always two or three lorries stacked high with the big bales of grass parked in the village, waiting to deliver their load and return to Granton, which at that time was the chief British port for the importation of this crop.

You leave the paved area of Main Street and climb past the lonely mill office, a sad but beautiful – in an

INFORMATION

Distance: 13.4 km (8.3 miles).

Map: OS Landranger, sheet 65.

Start and finish: Main Street, Balerno.

Terrain: Hilly byways. Much of the ride lies above the 200 m contour and can be exposed, even in summer. Be prepared: carry wind/waterproof clothing. Do not be afraid to turn back.

Refreshments: Only in Balerno.

Extensions: This route can be used as an extension of the Water of Leith ride (see Route 23).

The road from Balerno, with the Pentland hills in the distance.

View over Red Moss
Nature Reserve to the
Pentland hills.

industrial way – piece of architecture, continue up
Mansfield Road and head for the hills. There is relief
at Malleny Millgate, where you enter a region of
hedgeless open fields, but it still climbs, particularly
steeply at Upper Dean Park.

When you reach the top do not go straight on towards
the wildlife reserve, turn right at Red Moss and ride
along the northern fringes. Ian Finlay, in his splendid
book *The Lothians*, claims that the 'dark vistas of
heather and black peat hags might easily be in the
midst of Lewis or Sutherland', when he refers to the
moors where the Water of Leith has its source some 5
or 6 km to the west, but this patch is surely an outlier.
Caught in fading light it does not seem to belong here,
a shattered piece of the Highlands fallen in the wrong
place, but beautiful just the same.

Ride the long straight, mature trees on the right, the
moss on the left, the Pentlands across the fields, the
noise of birds on the western end of the reservoir
always with you. The trees look like an avenue that
has been filled in by strays, but becomes deliberately
dense at the western end. The roadside ditch runs with
clean water, no doubt a haven for frogs and newts, but
at the end of the road turn your back on the Pentlands
and head north on another beech-lined avenue. This
is obviously the main road. There is no signpost. These
are some of the most gnarled beech trees you will ever
see, the Scots pines looking much more at home.

There is a tremendous swoop down past Cockburnhill Farm, then turn left into Cockburn Hill Road. Strange to see a street sign in the midst of the country, even if it is hidden in the wrong verge for you, then follow the uphill undulations through Buteland to the triangle with the warning of a ford ahead. After turning right you will see the white bridge at the dry ford, but watch out for mossy deposits in any case.

The actual dark vistas of heather lie off to your left, although the watershed is so indeterminate that an old minister at Dolphinton once claimed that it was possible for a salmon to come up from the Tweed by this route and go down into the Clyde!

When you reach the A70, the infamous 'Lang Whang', turn right opposite the old American airfield, then right off it for Whelpside at the first opportunity. The Lang Whang was an old stage-coach route – the fantastic names live on. Little Vantage, the farm you pass, Boll o Bere, and a little further away an inn called Jenny's Toll, where two resurrection men took rest and refreshment while the bodies they had stolen from Lanark kirkyard for the anatomists in Edinburgh waited under a load of peats and straw on the cart outside. However, the corpses were rescued and reinterred by a posse from Currie. It is not recorded what happened to the body snatchers.

Some of the farm buildings at Glenbrook are in the process of stylish refurbishment, then there is a vehicle belonging a sidecar racing team lodged in the yard at Bankhead House. Definite signs of civilisation. The road delivers you to the outskirts of Balerno, and all that is required is to turn left and return to the start point.

Cottage in a picturesque setting on the outskirts of Balerno.

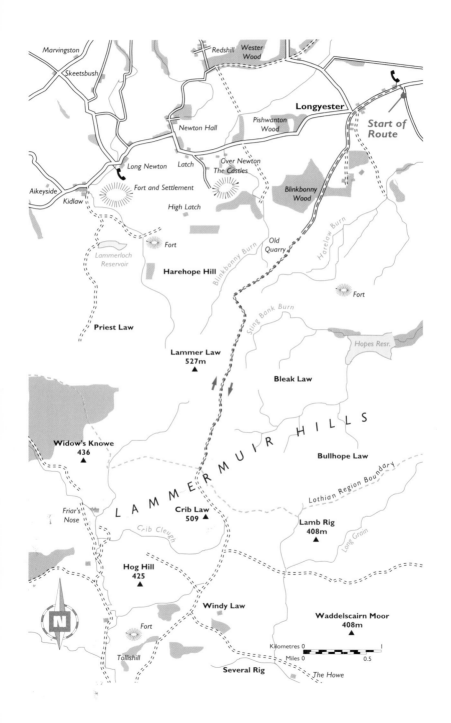

LAMMER LAW

The Lammermuir Hills form the backdrop to all the routes in East Lothian and several in Midlothian too. You may have skirted the northern slopes on earlier routes, a couple even probing a little, but this old coaching road over Lammer Law, 527 m, strikes straight through their heart. It has been said that if Soutra was the gate of Lothian, then Lammer Law is the gatepost. The more obvious reason for the 20th-century development in favour of Soutra is the fact that, despite the snow gates on the A68, it is 144 m lower, a major factor in keeping the modern winter traffic moving. Today you will climb to 507 m.

Strangely, despite its name, Lammer Law is not the highest hill in the range that bears its name. Meikle Says Law, about 5 km to the east is 8 m higher, but also lies on the Lothian border.

Although the River Tweed is oft regarded as the true Scottish Border, many scholars have voiced the opinion that it was actually the Lammermuir Hills that presented the last great obstacle to invading armies.

Even in summer these brown acres with steep-sided cleuchs can still be intimidating and, short as it is, this ride should be treated with respect. The weather up on the tops can be considerably different to that in which you start the ride, so go prepared: even on the brightest day take a windproof. The name Lammer is almost certainly associated with the word lamb. Sheep farming is, and always has been, the most important element of the economy in these high pastures, and throughout the Lammermuirs you will find names directly connected with sheep. Hogs Law and Hogs Rig (a hog being a yearling), Ewelairs Hill, Wedder Law, Wether Law, Wedderlie and Wedder Lair (a wedder or wether being a castrated ram), and of course there is Lamb Hill, Lamblair and Lamb Rig. This is most definitely sheep country.

INFORMATION

Distance: 11.0 km (6.8 miles)

Map: OS Landranger, sheet 66. Alternative start, sheet 65.

Start and finish: Hopes Road, near Longyester. Alternative start in Gifford to approach Longyester from the north. This adds 5.0 km (3.1 miles) to the route.

Terrain: Tarmac byways to begin, but the heart of the route lies over an old coaching road with an unsealed surface. Mountain bike terrain. Carry wind/waterproof clothing

Refreshments: None en route, unless you use the extension to Carfrae Mill, where meals are available at the hotel. Picnic recommended.

Extensions: The coaching road runs through the Lammermuirs to Carfrae Mill, Borders Region. The return distance from Longyester to Carfrae Mill is 27.8 km (17.3 miles), of which 13.7 km (8.5 miles) is tarmac. No convenient return route exists to make this a circular tour, the other crossing of the Lammermuirs in these parts being the A68 trunk road over Soutra. One solution would be to leave a vehicle at Carfrae Mill.

The signpost at Longyester.

Longyester (see Route 12) is a large, busy farm so the route starts nominally at the telephone box to the east. There is more room to park in the road to the Hopes, and this short extra distance will warm your legs through before you start to climb. Although this is the only true mountain bike route in the book, in the sense that some of the terrain is very uneven, a chance to get your legs moving on smoother roads before you hit the rough stuff should never be turned down. It avoids undue strain on cold muscles and gives you the opportunity to listen to your bike and confirm that all is well before other matters take precedence.

Ride west to Longyester and go straight on at the most oddly shaped crossroads in Scotland. Even the straight-on instruction is open to interpretation. The way you want is guarded by a 'No Through Road' sign but there is an old signpost partially hidden in the trees. It is worth a look. In non-metric designation the relevant arm reads: Lammerlaw 2.75 miles
Carfrae Mill 8.5 miles
Lauder 12.25 miles
Impassable for motors

Irresistible for mountain bikers, absolutely irresistible.

You can tell this is harsh countryside by the permanent corrugated iron lambing pens, supplemented by the usual straw bale windbreaks at the relevant time of year. But here the shepherd is obviously well used to lambing storms of some severity in April and May. The tarmac ends at a hazardous one-hinged gate. But here the navigational decision is easy. It is up, on the rough.

Take note of the track. Some of the old road is firm and compacted; some of it is loose. Choose the smoothest, and probably the easiest route, weaving across from side to side if necessary and trying to remember the best line for the return journey, when you will be going a lot faster. You will forget of course, but what it does achieve is focussing your attention on the fact there is considerable variation in different parts of this one track, and some good smooth lines do exist. Always search for the best.

Heather burning is evident all the way up the climb. Grouse need young tender shoots to eat; the burning is one way of ensuring that. A well-managed moor will look like a patchwork quilt, with a mixture of young and mature heather, the youngest for food, the oldest for nesting cover.

The old Haddington-Lauder road from high on the flanks of Lammer Law.

After all the initial toil, over the brow of the hill the road drops into the bowl at the head of the Harelaw Burn. This is not unusual, although never popular, on moorland routes, but there is the reassurance of seeing the road climbing the side of Harehope Hill in front of you. Do not veer left towards the corrugated shed, even if the track seems slightly smoother it only lasts 200 m.

The line of your road can be seen sweeping left immediately above the grassy slopes at the head of the bowl, the dividing line between pasture and moor. The road becomes compacted grass in places, which can be quite hazardous when descending in wet conditions. Take note of the locations. Then there is a brief glimpse of the star-shaped Hopes Reservoir before it becomes hidden again among the cleuchs.

If you have saved this route until last you will see many of the salient features of other routes when you pause as you climb: Traprain Law, North Berwick Law, Bass Rock, the Hopetoun Monument beyond Haddington, and the Firth of Forth. Do your sightseeing on the way up: you will need all your concentration on the way down. Then, quite suddenly, between the gates, the road starts to go down again. You have reached the top.

Public Right of Way sign on the old Haddington-Lauder road.

The Lothian border sits on the col beyond the second gate, at the track junction. This is the turnaround point. Unless you are pressing on to Carfrae Mill, which is reached by simply following the main track, retrace to the last gate and reap the rewards of your labours with a splendid ride back down, taking care on the steep descent.

PUBLIC RIGHT OF WAY
LAUDER-HADDINGTON

IN THE INTEREST OF
CONSERVATION PLEASE KEEP
TO THE PATH AND KEEP DOGS
ON A LEAD   F.E.L.

FURTHER INFORMATION

For further information on cycling in Lothian, contact:

Freephone:
      Clarence 0800 232323

or write to:
      Transportation Department
      18–19 Market Street
      Edinburgh
      EH1 1BL

Opposite: A typically peaceful Lothian scene.

INDEX

HMSO

HMSO Bookshops
71 Lothian Road, Edinburgh EH3 9AZ
0131-228 4181 Fax 0131-229 2734
49 High Holborn, London WC1V 6HB
(counter service only)
0171-873 0011 Fax 0171-831 1326
68–69 Bull Street, Birmingham B4 6AD
0121-236 9696 Fax 0121-236 9699
33 Wine Street, Bristol BS1 2BQ
0117 9264306 Fax 0117 9294515
9-21 Princess Street, Manchester M60 8AS
0161-834 7201 Fax 0161-833 0634
16 Arthur Street, Belfast BT1 4GD
01232 238451 Fax 01232 235401
The HMSO Oriel Bookshop, The Friary, Cardiff
CF1 4AA
01222 395548 Fax 01222 384347

HMSO publications are available from:

HMSO Publications Centre
(Mail, fax and telephone orders only)
PO Box 276, London SW8 5DT
Telephone orders 0171-873 9090
General enquiries 0171-873 0011
(queuing system in operation for both numbers)
Fax orders 0171-873 8200

HMSO's Accredited Agents
(see Yellow Pages)

and through good booksellers